Fair **P9-BZP-862**

2198 Roaring Creek Road
Roan Mountain, TN 37687
423-772-4269

8^{00}

HE
GIVETH
MORE
GRACE

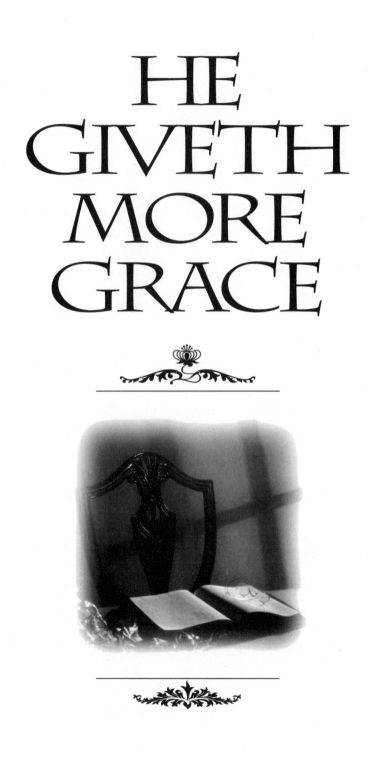

Endorsements

The heart of David Lynch's ministry beats with the tenderness of Calvary. His deep love, respect, and reverence for God's Word, combined with his gifts of bring a measure of comprehension to the incomprehensible, unsearchable riches of Christ, remains the distinguishing characteristic of his life and ministry.

Randy Vader
PRESIDENT
PRAISE GATHERING MUSIC GROUP

David Lynch is one of the most encouraging and practical pastors of today. I have known David and his wife for several years now and their ministry together is one of honesty, comfort, and commitment. I know these writings will speak straight to the heart of every believer.

Shelly Chapin
EXECUTIVE DIRECTOR CSC MINISTRIES
MUSICIAN, FAMILY COUNSELOR, AND AUTHOR

Dave Lynch shares little jewels of wisdom and truth for those in need of divine riches. You will dip into the King's treasure as you journey through a devotional book designed to impart the Master's wealth to the children of His kingdom.

Lana Bateman
PRESIDENT
PHILIPPIAN MINISTRIES & AUTHOR

HE GIVETH MORE GRACE

A Thoughtful and Inspiring Collection of
Devotional Vignettes
that Share the Peace, Joy, and Abundance of
the Christian Life.

David Lynch

FOREWORD BY GLORIA GAITHER

Star Song Publishing Group, a division of Jubilee Communications, Inc.,
2325 Crestmoor, Nashville, Tennessee 37215.
Printed in the United States of America.

Cover photography by David Bailey.
Cover and interior design by Synnöve Inman.

First Printing, October 1994
1 2 3 4 5 6 7 8 9 10 — 99 98 97 96 95 94

Introduction

Early in my pastoral ministry, I began writing a devotional article for the weekly church newsletter. I have continued that practice for the past thirty-six years. My purpose was to bring a word of comfort and encouragement to those whom I serve. Over the years, many of those who received the newsletter have said, "You ought to publish these." I heard from lay people and pastors alike that the articles spoke to them and also provided them with ideas to use in their sermons or when they had to lead devotions. That is my purpose in finally putting some of the writings into this book.

First, I sincerely hope the Spirit will use these devotionals to speak to you in your present circumstances. I have attempted to speak to the issues we all face on a regular basis. Hopefully, you will find strength and encouragement to face life victoriously. Second, some articles may provide you with a sermon illustration or a devotional thought the next time you stand before a group in your church or in another setting. If so, the ministry of this book has been enlarged.

These writings come from my heart to yours. They grow out of personal experiences that have taught me how real God is in the arena of everyday life. In the past six years, my wife has triumphed over cancer and I have learned to live with heart disease, so we know something of the uncertainty of life. We have also discovered that God is faithful and His mercies are new every morning! That is the message I want to share—if Christ is for us, it really doesn't matter who or what is against us *(Rom. 8:31)*.

David Lynch

OCTOBER 1994

Foreword

He isn't bombastic, theatrical, or the epitome of a salesman. And he hasn't built mega-churches, created gargantuan metropolitan ministries, or amassed a fleet of Sunday School buses. In fact, he is a surprising person for God to have chosen to be a leader in a culture and time that puts a premium on powerful personalities and instant successes.

If I had to find adjectives to describe him they would tend to be words like *shy, consistent, unobtrusive, humble,* and *serious.* So why this good, quiet man is the pastor of a vibrant, thriving community of caring persons in a university town, I really can't say.

All I know is that God has, down through history, had a habit of picking unlikely, surprising men and women to accomplish the work of the Kingdom on this earth. Moses stuttered, Abraham got in a hurry, Jacob came to blows with an angel, Miriam sided with the dissenters, David messed up with a woman. Zacharias made fun of God's idea and John the Baptist was crude.

Suffice it to say, that about the time we come up with the prototype for the job description, God has a way of blowing our plans out of the water.

So every Sunday, I sit in the fourth pew on the left side of the church with my husband, my children, their friends and spouses, and our new grandbaby. Together we listen to our unlikely pastor as he oh, so rightly "divides the Word of truth." He holds our hands when we sit in the waiting room of surgery, he stands by us in prayer for our kids, and a few months ago he spread his arms around our whole family as we sobbed out our grief for the "letting go" of my precious mother who died of cancer.

And somehow I know that these thoughts that come from the heart of this unlikely great man will change the chemistry and focus of our days. Knowing God, why should that surprise me?

Gloria Gaither

Dedication

To Wanda,

my partner, sweetheart, best friend, and

companion of forty-two years.

Her enthusiasm for life, her commitment

to Christ, and her devotion

to prayer have been a constant source of

strength and encouragement.

Acknowledgments

"How can I say thanks?" Where does one begin to offer thanks for all who have contributed so much to my life and the publication of this book?

Let me begin by thanking my wife, Wanda, who has encouraged me for years to write a book; and to my cousin Freida who also refused to stop pushing until the task was completed.

I want to thank my secretary, Marv Carey, who had the unenviable task of reading my writing and putting it in printed form.

Thanks also to my friend Leland Boren who holds my feet to the fire and causes me to constantly set my sights higher.

Further thanks to Gloria Gaither for writing the foreword. She is a faithful friend whom I admire and respect deeply.

Thanks to Shelley Chapin for allowing me to use several articles previously published in *Rhythms of the Heart*, a devotional book she edited for Victor Books.

Thanks to Gaither Music Company for permission to use the song, "Should the Harvest Never Come."

This book could not have been written without the people in the churches I have pastored, whose walk with Christ has impacted my faith and provided the basis for many of the articles.

Finally, sincere thanks to Matthew Price and the staff at Star Song for their help and encouragement.

Called By Name

The watchman opens the gate for him,
and the sheep listen to his voice.
He calls his own sheep by name and leads them out.
When he has brought out all his own,
he goes ahead of them, and his sheep follow him
because they know his voice.

JOHN 10:3–4

When someone calls my name, it gets my attention! And I answer those to whom I belong.

I remember my mother calling me to come home at supper time. I could tell by the tone in her voice how quickly I needed to respond! There was no doubt in my mind who she was speaking to or what she wanted. I belonged to her! And she knew me well.

When teachers called my name growing up, I responded (sometimes with fear if I wasn't prepared that day!). They knew me and I belonged in their classrooms. They got my attention.

Now I have been married for years, and my wife has a special way of calling my name. She can say "David" in a way that no one else can! And often I know what she wants or what she's thinking simply by the sound of her voice.

One of our greatest needs is to belong. And one of the most amazing truths of Scripture is that God knows us by name! We belong to God. He knows the hairs on our heads, our thoughts before we think them, the steps we will take, and the fears we harbor. The God of the universe knows each of us intimately.

How grateful I am that I heard Him say, many years ago,

"David, I love you and I sent My Son to die for your sins. I want to forgive you. You belong to Me." He knew me and He sought me out and He gave me life. I belong to my Heavenly Father.

Since that time, He has continued to know and call my name. "David, I know you are hurting." "David, I want you to help this person for Me." "David, take this step of faith and trust Me." "David, My grace is sufficient for you to make it through this valley." I still belong to God, and I always will.

Almighty God knows my name. And He knows your name too. If you listen carefully, you'll hear His voice telling you how much He loves and cares for you.

God knows what you're dealing with. He knows and is aware of your needs. His love can bring courage and forgiveness and a reminder that you, too, belong.

We want to belong, but there are so many voices telling us how to live, what to choose, and where to belong that we tend to get confused. We become sidetracked by the priorities and expectations of the world.

Remember that there is only One to whom you truly belong. There is only one voice which speaks the truth and He never leads us astray.

Choose to belong. It is a gift that is offered to you and to me. And it isn't a temporary condition! We belong to a loving and gracious Heavenly Father for eternity.

The Rest Jesus Offers

The LORD *replied,*
"My Presence will go with you, and I will give you rest."
EXODUS 33:14

Weary . . . burdened . . . broken. Can you identify with those terms? Most of us can at one time or another. In fact, even as I write I can think of friends who are carrying a load that is heavy right now.

I think of Greg who spent many, many days at the hospital by his wife's side. Away from home and tired, they faced one battle after another. How broken they must have felt in the turmoil.

I think of some dear friends in Cleveland. My wife and I have shared wonderful times of fellowship with them over the years. They are like family. We have laughed and cried, prayed and planned together.

A massive stroke changed everything. The husband entered a nursing home, no longer able to speak or respond to his dear wife. And no longer can we laugh or cry or pray or plan in the manner we had depended on for years. What anguish the family has suffered! How weary and burdened his wife has felt. The life that they knew was broken apart.

I think of children who struggle with the pain of divorce. I think of wives who suffer the agony of abuse. I think of lives enslaved to alcohol or drugs. I think of the internal strife in their neighborhoods or countries.

Yes, there are many broken and weary people in our world. Some of them occupy the seats right next to you or me on Sunday morning. Sometimes *we* are the brokenhearted in need of understanding and hope.

Is there hope? Can we do anything to make the world better? Where can people turn for the mending of wounded hearts and broken spirits?

"Come to me, all you who are weary and burdened, and I will give you rest" (Matt. 11:28). I love those words spoken by Jesus. Rest—such a wonderful prospect in the midst of our pain.

The rest Jesus offers is not necessarily the removal of the problem. The rest is not always a quick solution. The rest is not always the physical healing we desire or the removal of the source of our pain.

Rest is there for our weary spirits. I cannot tell you exactly when or how our Lord gives this rest, I simply know that He does—in His own time and in His own way. Right in the midst of our personal storm, the Father brings comfort.

I am so thankful that our Lord understands our weariness. He was weary too. He experienced rejection, loneliness, abuse, unreliable friends, and the myriad of other pains we undergo. Jesus knew what it was to be weary and to need some kind of renewal and communion.

Our Lord sees when we are weary. He knows the ache in our heart and the pain of the struggle. He understands what makes us anxious and burdened. He says, "Bring it to Me! Cry it out. Tell Me exactly how you feel. Let go and express your emotions—you can be honest with Me. Then, let Me take you in My arms and give you rest!"

The Tender Taming of Our Egos

*All of you, clothe yourselves with humility
toward one another, because,
"God opposes the proud but gives grace to the humble."*
1 PETER 5:5B

Fred Smith is a successful Christian businessman who has spent years of his life as a consultant to many of the top corporations in our nation. Someone asked him once how he goes in to such corporate giants as General Motors or IBM and discovers the problem.

"That's easy," he replied. "I just look for the ego. When I find the ego, I know where the problem lies."

When I stopped to ponder Mr. Smith's response, I realized that the same thing can be said about any company, regardless of size. This can also be said of churches, school systems, sports teams, marriages, and almost any relationship!

At the crux of most of our problems lies the simple statement (usually unspoken), "I want my way." The desire is at the very core of our human, carnal nature. It is a reality known to us all.

I would like to say that becoming a Christian automatically removes the carnality and ego-battles, but I have been in the church too long to be so naive! When we come to Christ, our sins are forgiven and we begin the process of growth. But that process is one which continues throughout our Christian life; it is not a transformation that is instant and complete.

The Holy Spirit is constantly at work in the life of the believer, breaking down all of those barriers to maturity. If we allow Him entrance and cooperate with Him, He works to cleanse us of the effects of sin and give us victory over the ego we are generally so comfortable protecting.

Like Mr. Smith, the Holy Spirit knows He has to go to the source of our problem—the ego. Even the apostle Paul had to deal with that issue. He confessed that he had to die to himself daily. He had to experience crucifixion of his own ambitions and self-sufficiency. The Paul-life had to gradually give way to the Christ-life.

Am I demanding my own way? Am I expecting others to change in ways that I am unwilling to change or compromise? Have I developed blind spots that will not allow me to see my own areas of need? Do I think I am so spiritual that I no longer need accountability? Am I willing to take responsibility for my actions and humbly say, "I'm sorry. I've been wrong. Please forgive me"?

These are tough questions, I know. And it is tough to answer them honestly! But the answers just might help us to discover where we need that tender taming of our own wills.

Allow the Holy Spirit the privilege of gently yet persistently breaking you of the ego-controls. Those who are broken and humble make such a difference in the world around them. Marriages and families are healthier, relationships at work are more gratifying and, in general, life as a believer is far more satisfying and whole when we allow ourselves to be broken and open to maturity.

The ego is quite a large obstacle! And it certainly can be stubborn. Yet think about the growth that is available to every believer through the ministry of the Spirit.

Supernatural Power

*Not that we are competent in ourselves to
claim anything for ourselves, but our competence comes from God.*
2 CORINTHIANS 3:5

Once, after I had preached a message on prayer, a university student wrote, "I just wanted to let you know that your statement, 'prayer can do anything God can do,' has made a tremendous impact on my life. Somehow I always thought that prayer shared my limitations instead of God's power."

This honest individual is not the only one who comes to God more aware of human limitations than of God's power. For many of us, our relationship with God often becomes a matter of human effort. We find ourselves saying, "Maybe if I pray long enough or hard enough, God will answer." We struggle with who's in charge. And we often attempt to take control.

The truth is, we could pray for two hours and work up a "holy sweat" and be no closer to experiencing God's power than before. The focus of power and control is the One to whom we pray and on whom we depend. It is not the effort itself that gets results. It is the response of the Heavenly Father to the simple, childlike trust of a Christian who believes that God can do anything.

When I look at the needs around me—the decaying society in which we live and the awesome mission to which God has called us—I feel terribly inadequate. I am out of control, but God is not.

How thankful I am that the results of life in this world are not dependent on my skills and abilities. How grateful I am for the promises of Scripture that enable me to come to the Father knowing that He hears me and is able to do far more than I can even think or ask. What a blessed relief to know that the outcome is in His hands.

Good news, friend! God is in control, so you can resign. It is not by might or by power or human effort, but by the Spirit of the living God that prayer becomes effective. God is in control.

God of the Impossible

We are hard pressed on every side, but not crushed;
perplexed, but not in despair; persecuted,
but not abandoned; struck down, but not destroyed.
2 CORINTHIANS 4:8–9

Pressures. Stress. Burnout. Frustration. Despair. Fear. All of these are realities that we live with daily—realities that are quite frequently beyond our control, despite our fervent attempts!

Do you know anyone who doesn't battle with these enemies of emotional and physical health? And which one of us doesn't become spiritually weary under excessive stress and pressure?

We like to think of the apostle Paul as that unbeatable servant of God—impossible to stop and positive beyond reproach. Paul was, indeed, God's servant. But Paul wasn't protected from the stresses and strains which face us all during our time in this world.

We need only to examine Paul's letters to the Corinthians to remember he knew more than his share of stress and despair. He wrote that "we despaired even of life" and "in our hearts we felt the sentence of death" (2 Cor. 1:8–9). Paul knew pain, and he shared his pain openly.

How can we deal with the stresses of life? When we feel out of control, what can we do to regain composure? What can become our help in those times when we seem overwhelmed?

The answer is simple, but certainly not easy to pursue. It seems that Paul's answer to despair was to go to God. The impossible situations he and his friends faced led them into the presence of the One who can do the impossible. God rescued them, as only He can do, from the need to control what wasn't under their dominion.

I remember a story of Corrie ten Boom. She'd been taught by a friend a secret for handling despair. "When you face a problem that seems impossible, go to a mirror, gaze at yourself, and say, 'Lord Jesus, I've a problem that You cannot handle. It is way too big for You.' Then wait and see what happens."

Corrie's response was usually a laugh. Realizing her desire to control the uncomfortable, she would laugh, commit the need to God, and receive His rest. Simple, but not always easy.

When we turn to God with our needs, stresses, fears, and feelings of despair, He steps in and takes control. He delivered Paul from the need to worry, and He'll do the same for you and for me.

Perhaps you're facing stress beyond your ability to endure. Perhaps you're feeling out of control from all life's pressures.

Try what Corrie suggested. Try what seemed to work for Paul and his friends. Turn to God, and let Him take the lead.

"I've Fallen, But I Can Get Up!"

"So do not fear, for I am with you;
do not be dismayed, for I am your God. I will strengthen you and
help you; I will uphold you with my righteous right hand."
ISAIAH 41:10

We've all seen the television commercial that made an unknown elderly woman famous! She is lying on the floor saying the well-remembered line, "I've fallen and I can't get up!"

The thing that makes the commercial humorous is the fact that it is so obviously staged! We all know the woman didn't really fall, and so we laugh. But if this were a real-life situation, we would not be laughing at all.

For many people, the cry, "I've fallen and I can't get up" is a brutal reality. They have not fallen physically, but the sense of not being able to get up out of the circumstance that holds them down is very real.

Some have fallen beneath a load of sin. It was a gradual fall. Everything seemed so innocent in the beginning. But the wages of sin is always death of some kind. They now sit down to a banquet of consequences, and life looks hopeless.

Some have fallen into habits that destroy and degrade. They find themselves trapped in a lifestyle of compulsive behavior over which they no longer have control. They never thought it could happen to them, but it *has* happened. And there seems to be no way out.

26

Some have fallen financially. The job that once held so much promise is gone. Or habits of spending have gotten out of hand. Bills are piling up. Self-esteem is at an all-time low. They're sure if they see any light at the end of the tunnel it will be a train.

I have some good news for you and for me. God says that we *can* get up. As bad as the situation looks right now, God's grace is greater than our need. Christ came to break the power of sin and suffering so that no matter how far we have fallen, He can lift us up, transform our lives, and give us a new start. It simply takes a little bit of courage on our part to reach out and grasp hold of His grace.

If you find yourself under the weight of unemployment or divorce, disability or grief, you are not alone. If you find yourself single with no change in sight or discouraged about school or a job, you are not alone.

It is the enemy who whispers in your ear, "You can't get up. Just accept defeat." It is Jesus who says, "You *can* get up! You can do all things through the strength I will give you." Failure is never the last word. Financial problems do have solutions. Broken relationships can result in healing or understanding. And you are already forgiven, reconciled, and adopted as children into God's family.

I am not saying that the pain will end or that you'll no longer feel discouraged. Nor am I trying to downplay the reality of our suffering. What I *am* saying is that Jesus helps us in everything. There is no problem or habit, no sin or suffering that goes beyond His commitment to help.

You may have fallen—we all do. But you can get up! Simply reach out, take a step, call for help. God will grant you courage— the strength and grace sufficient for the journey.

Coping with Life's Unfairness

Then they cried to the LORD in their trouble,
and he saved them from their distress.
PSALM 107:13

I'll never forget one particular meal. I was seated at a nice restaurant eating my broiled fish like a good cholesterol-watcher, when I noticed a man at the table next to me. He was older than I, much heavier, and he was wolfing down clam chowder, fried fish, fried shrimp, french fries, and chocolate cake!

That just isn't fair, I thought. *I am hungry, and this guy gets to eat all the food!*

In case you haven't noticed, life isn't fair. And the Bible never promises that life will be fair. Our problem is that sometimes we confuse life with God and we accuse Him of being unfair.

It helps to remember that life is not God. Simply because life deals us tragedy, affliction, or problems we can't handle does not mean that God is picking on us or is uninterested in our well-being.

Still, in the midst of our sufferings we certainly feel disappointment. And we are in good company. Job, Jeremiah, and John were all disappointed in life and they spoke openly to God about their frustration.

I, too, have felt disappointed with God in a very personal area. For a period of time my wife, Wanda, suffered from cancer of the kidney, and I don't need to tell you how difficult it was for me to stand by and not be able to fix her pain.

28

Many people who face debilitating illnesses like cancer grow weary and angry with God. Though anger did not pose a problem for Wanda, she did wrestle with some very real fears in the course of her illness. She lived one day at a time, praying to trust God's love and power, even in the midst of her sorrow.

Jesus said that in this world we will have trouble, and He was right! Why some bad things happen to some good people I do not know.

What I do know is that God has promised never to forsake us. Even through our disappointments, we have the guarantee of God's sufficient grace.

When faced with disappointment, hold on to God's unchanging hand. He is there, and He will provide the strength, the mercy, and the grace to grow through the suffering.

The Importance of Discipline

*Now it is required that those who
have been given a trust must prove faithful.*
1 CORINTHIANS 4:2

While walking along the beach in southern Florida, one sees some unusual sights! As I took my morning walk, I observed people of all sizes, shapes, and age-groups and I was impressed. Most of the people much older than I were taking walking *seriously*! They were not out for a leisurely stroll along the water; they were working with great dedication.

I was walking at a good pace myself (or so I thought!) until a couple of seventy-five-year-old ladies passed me by! Then I began to take notice! I even watched as some men went the length of the beach several times. They did so with the commitment of one who is training for a marathon race!

Have you ever considered how important discipline is to the Christian life? We often talk about God's faithfulness, but we rarely talk about our own. Yet if we expect to grow in faith and become strong, it takes some responsibility and faithfulness on our part.

God doesn't wake us up and knock us out of bed in the morning and say, "Get up and pray!" Nor does He tie us into a chair and say, "You're not getting up until you read the Bible!" He doesn't even give us a wake-up call so that we won't miss church or Bible study. God respects our decisions.

I wish good marriages automatically happened, but they don't. I wish God would leave a sermon on my desk each Thursday, but He doesn't. I wish we could be good parents simply by wanting to be, but that's not the way the system works!

The apostle Paul knew this secret about faithfulness. He understood that just because of his calling or the great things God had done through his ministry, there was no coasting! He had to work at keeping his relationship with the Lord fresh. He had to keep running the race (see 1 Cor. 9:24–27). He had to remain faithful to that which he had begun.

To be faithful to God is to offer Him a great gift. This doesn't mean that we have to pretend to like everything that happens. It doesn't mean that we shouldn't cry or struggle or question. Faithfulness to God is a commitment to trust His leading and to act on that which we know to be true about Him.

Don't wait for some "zap" from heaven to make life perfect. Don't look for an emotional experience to bring you to spiritual maturity.

God has given us a Book and a living example of life-changing principles. Let's commit to following faithfully that which He has provided.

If you need some inspiration, go to a beach or a mall and watch some senior citizens walk! Or focus on men and women like Paul, Daniel, Joseph, Hannah, Esther, and Ruth. It is a privilege to offer God the blessed gift of faithfulness.

Calm in the Storm

"Peace I leave with you; my peace I give you.
I do not give to you as the world gives.
Do not let your hearts be troubled and do not be afraid."
JOHN 14:27

I have no idea what kinds of things move you to fear, but I can tell you that there are several situations which are sure to inspire fear in me. One of those fear-inspirers for me is found high in the sky, up above all other movement. I am not a great fan of flying.

Though not exactly enamored with the idea, I said yes one day when a church member offered to fly me and a friend to a nearby town for lunch. The appointment day came and the sky was blue, so I felt relieved. After all, blue skies and bright sun make for a perfect flying day, right? Not exactly!

I soon learned that a low cloud cover causes turbulence and that even though the sky is blue, the air can be quite bumpy. As we took off for our getaway, the pilot advised that the ride would be rough, and rough it was. As the small plane bounced and swayed, I held on tightly to the armrest. I felt fear, but as I gazed at the face of my pilot friend, I knew he was assured. The one in charge was not at all disturbed by the turbulence.

Our bumpy ride that day reminded me of one boat ride taken by the disciples and our Lord. Everything was fine until the storm hit, then all of the disciples grew fearful and distraught. I can understand their anxiety, but Jesus didn't seem disturbed by the storm. He was asleep in the back of the boat, a fact I'm grateful was not duplicated in my airplane story! The more the disciples feared, the more frustrated they became with Jesus' seeming lack of sensitivity to the situation. How could He be so calm when they were experiencing such fear?

Our Lord was calm because He was in control. The storm didn't bother Him any more than a little turbulence worried my pilot friend. It was I and the disciples who let our fear get the best of us!

I relaxed a few times on the return trip, and I am trying to learn to relax on life's journey as well. There are many situations I can fear, but my fear belies a very important truth.

God is in control of our lives. The turbulent situations of life do not catch Him off guard. He is in control—always. And He never tires of graciously reminding us that He will not leave us or forsake us.

There is no storm we face that Jesus hasn't already weathered. He promises to accompany us through everything we experience. Perhaps this assurance can soothe our fears and provide us with calm in the midst of the storm.

Anything But Cheap

*For there is one God and one mediator between God and men,
the man Christ Jesus, who gave himself
as a ransom for all men—the testimony given in its proper time.*
1 TIMOTHY 2:5–6

American military presence in the Philippine Islands was being phased out. We had been there for years, yet now it was time for our power to fade. A chaplain and his family who had served there for some time began to prepare for departure.

"There is much we haven't yet seen," they decided. "Let's spend our final days visiting the sights we've put off until now." The plan seemed like a good one.

It was Easter Sunday, not long after the family had made their resolution. The chaplain conducted four services and then put the children into the car to head for downtown Manila. They wanted to see the Easter celebration at the great cathedral, and they were just in time for the final portion.

They parked as close as possible and began to make their way toward the square. As they walked along, they passed vendors who were selling all kinds of religious merchandise: candles, incense, veils, rosaries, prayer books and, of course, jewelry. They could hardly believe all the trinkets that were available for purchase in the middle of such a great event.

As the family rounded the final corner toward their goal, a surprise awaited them. There stood a man adorned in crucifixes! Yes, draped on every available appendage and piece of clothing were crosses of all shapes and sizes.

"CHEAP CROSSES FOR SALE," read the hand-lettered sign, hung crudely around the man's neck. "Cheap crosses sold here."

Can you imagine such a message, and on Easter! As if a cross could somehow be construed as "a bargain."

There was nothing cheap about the cross borne by our Lord. It was an instrument of death, stained with blood and marked by the nails in His hands and feet. There was no bargain there.

In order to offer forgiveness, the price Jesus paid was immense. There is no human way to imagine, much less describe, the burden carried by our Lord. And yet He chose to carry the load in order to offer forgiveness.

Jesus had already prepared His disciples for the meaning of the cross. He also extended the meaning to include those who would long to follow in His steps. "If anyone would come after me, he must deny himself, take up his cross daily and follow me" (Luke 9:23).

Is Jesus literally asking us to die on a cross? No. Nor is He suggesting that we strap ourselves to a piece of wood or carry a cross up a hill. Such an act could accomplish nothing—forgiveness is already ours!

Jesus is asking us to commit our lives to Him and to all that the cross meant and means. He is asking us to commit to forgiveness, reconciliation, and eternal perspectives. He is asking us to give up ownership to the only worthy Lord. He is asking us to align ourselves with His love and purposes.

Forgiveness is anything but cheap. It is the root of reconciliation and restoration; it is the foundation for Christianity. It is the great gift from our Lord that keeps on giving its gracious rewards.

We do not have "cheap crosses" or "cut-rate forgiveness" for sale. We have a Savior to share with the world whose love, death, resurrection, and life have set us free!

The Last Word

We have this hope as an anchor for the soul, firm and secure.
HEBREWS 6:19

If I had to choose one word to describe the benefit of Christianity that means the most to me, that word would be *hope*.

No matter what kind of situation we are forced to deal with, it is not hopeless. No matter how deep our sorrow might be, it is never the last word. And no matter how rebellious and far from God we or a loved one might stray, "hopeless" need never be used to describe the situation. With God, there is always hope.

Gethsemane was a terrible and agonizing experience for our Lord. None of us will ever know the depth of His pain nor the agonizing loneliness that accompanied His choice. And if we were to view that situation from the human perspective alone, we would see "hopeless" engraved on every heart and every expression of life that day.

On that Friday we call "good," there hung One who claimed to be God's Son. Positioned between two thieves while hundreds looked on, any hope of His being the Savior faded as nails held His hands to the cross. All of the dreams once shared by the disciples grew pale against the dark death of "the King of the Jews."

What happened? What went wrong? How could things have ended this way?

As hopeless as everything seemed, God always has the last word. Nothing ended that Friday; in fact, hope really began. And I smile to think of the look on their faces as person after person inspected the tomb and searched for a body once dead.

God took the most hopeless situation we will ever face and removed its sting. His victory became ours that day. And in such hope, I find great relief.

Whatever you're facing right now, no matter how impossible or hopeless it may seem, just remember Easter. Easter put hope into our lives to stay, and nothing this world offers can ever change that provision.

There is now a bright light in the tunnel of death. There is now a great good in the well of our suffering. And there is now infinite hope in the heart of every believer, there simply for the taking.

I'll rely on hope today. Someone will call to share deep pain. Someone will confess a wrong that's still not right. And somewhere in the midst of it all, I'll feel my own loneliness, weariness, or frustration. Yet hope will be my companion and my grateful reminder that we are His. The same power that raised Christ from the dead is at work in you and me.

A Matter of Life and Life

*"I tell you the truth, whoever hears my word and believes
him who sent me has eternal life and
will not be condemned; he has crossed over from death to life."*
JOHN 5:24

I'll never forget the day I learned that a close friend of mine had been diagnosed with terminal cancer. How does one deal with such devastating news? How does one begin to cope when time is no longer an expectation?

Though the news sent all of us who love my friend reeling, it was the man himself who taught us how to see this suffering. When discussing whether or not to take chemotherapy and radiation treatments, he said to me, "Dave, this isn't a matter of life and death; it's a matter of life and life!"

He is right! Imagine such a thought coming from someone who's actually facing that reality. Either way my friend wins, but such hope is difficult for us to grasp.

Paul describes the journey of hope in his second recorded letter to the Corinthians. In summary the apostle said, "If we die, we're really trading in this earthly body for a heavenly one!" (see 5:1–5). What a testimony to the hope of the gospel! Christians don't surrender life for death; we exchange earthly life for eternal life!

What crosses your mind when Paul writes the word *tent*? Security? Comfort? Permanence? No! Tents are none of these things. They were never intended to be permanent dwellings. And neither are these bodies of ours!

Paul likens our earthly bodies to temporary tents to remind us that living here is not the grand finale. Death, for the Christian, is the point of "exchange." Once we move into our new house, we can unpack and throw away every encumbrance we've ever known.

In short, death for the believer is a continuation of the life we have found in Christ. Our Lord said, "I have come so that they might have life" (John 10:10)—life that never ends. This is the essence of hope.

You may be struggling now with all kinds of difficulties and losses. Try to remember hope. No matter what we face, the choice is life and *life*.

Washing Feet

*God is not unjust; he will not forget your work and
the love you have shown him as
you have helped his people and continue to help them.*
HEBREWS 6:10

In the thirteenth chapter of John's Gospel, Jesus is seen doing a very strange thing. Instead of acting like a leader in the traditional sense, He takes the role of a servant. We are told that He demonstrated the full extent of His love by washing the feet of His disciples.

Why did Jesus wash their feet? Why did He choose this humble act to communicate loving leadership?

Jesus left His disciples not only with teachings to follow, but with an example to live by. He didn't want to just tell them to love one another, He wanted to show them how. And He wanted them to experience the privilege of servanthood and know their worth in His eyes.

Leona is one of the faithful servants of the world. She and her sister Elsie were members of the first congregation we pastored. I was new to the ministry and anxious to exhibit the love and servanthood of our Lord, but I wasn't too sure just how such love and servanthood should be exhibited!

Leona and Elsie lived in a small frame house with none of the modern conveniences. Water for cooking and washing had to be carried in from the pump. But Leona was a gracious host and insisted we sit at her table. Both Wanda and I counted it a joy to be served by this loving woman.

Elsie was mentally handicapped and she needed a caring guardian. Long ago, Leona had chosen to be that person. She never married. She never pursued her own dreams. She chose, instead, to devote her life to caring for her sister.

Sometimes the road got rough and she would call for help or comfort, but most of the time Leona simply loved her sister, literally "washing her feet" and caring for her needs. Such love is hard to come by.

Jesus could have chosen a more visible role. He could have insisted on obedience and a powerful position. He could have demanded that the disciples wash *His* feet. But that is not the path our Lord wanted to walk.

Jesus had a message to share and to live, and that message was simple: "Love one another as I have loved you. Serve one another as I have served you." The two go hand in hand.

Leona didn't write a book or lead a conference or serve on any committees. And I doubt if she ever acquired many of the modern conveniences. Leona spent her whole life washing the feet of one she loved. And few even noticed. She showed the full extent of her love each day as she set aside her own rights for those of an unaware sister.

A Piece of the Rock

LORD, you establish peace for us;
all that we have accomplished you have done for us.
ISAIAH 26:12

When a child in our church had outpatient surgery one day, I learned something about praying with young children and I learned something important about peace.

I remember trying to pray in terms I thought my young friend would understand. I thanked Jesus for being David's friend. I prayed for the doctors who would be performing the surgery. And then I prayed that God would give David a peace while he waited for the surgery to begin.

What I did not know until later was this. When I prayed for "a peace," little David opened his eyes, looked at his mother standing near, and mouthed, "A piece of what?" As his mother related the story to me, we both had a good laugh.

Later, after the surgery had gone well and David was resting, I pondered the misunderstanding which had earlier clouded my prayer. Two things occurred to me.

First, I decided not to pray that prayer with a small child again! But, second I realized that when we trust our lives to the Lord we have both "peace" and "a piece"! This is what I mean.

When we trust our lives to Jesus Christ, we have "a piece" of the Rock! God's grace lifts us out of the kingdom of darkness and places us into the kingdom of light. A piece of everything that belongs to Christ belongs to us—everything!

Is that fantastic or what? You and I own a piece of heaven! We have access to God's storehouse of riches! We belong to God's for-ever family. And if I read Scripture correctly, our rooms in God's mansion will be debt-free. There will be no taxes, no utilities, no repairs, and no mortgages. Hallelujah!

We also have peace when we trust our lives to the Lord; we don't have to wait for heaven to experience this part of God's gift. Peace is a promise from God, a deep reminder of our eternal belonging. Peace reminds us of the ministry and love of our Lord.

As Jesus prepared the disciples for His own death, He described the eternal blessings that would be theirs. And then He ended with a simple statement of purpose: "I have told you these things, so that in me you may have peace" (John 16:33).

I pray that as David grows older he will accept a piece of the Rock. And I pray that he will experience the peace that only the Rock can give.

Extrasensory Peace

And the peace of God, which transcends all understanding,
will guard your hearts and your minds in Christ Jesus.
PHILIPPIANS 4:7

There are those who claim to have extrasensory perception, or "ESP." In layman's terms, this is the ability to communicate mysteriously across the miles. Those who claim the ability may know what is happening to someone in another part of the world. They may dream that a certain person has died and then wake the next day to discover that the dream is indeed a reality. Or they may reveal the location of a lost article.

I don't know how to explain ESP except to acknowledge that there are experiences beyond our understanding. But there is another form of ESP I do understand because I have known its benefits time and time again.

I am talking about "Extrasensory Peace." It is a gift from God and it comes at just the right moment to fill our need. It is a peace that truly passes understanding and comes from a source way beyond our own senses.

Jesus promised us His peace when leaving this world and He kept His promise. He spoke peace on all who came to find rest, love, and healing, and He continues to speak peace. His is a supernatural peace that transcends understanding, and it is constant, even in the midst of life's most difficult circumstances.

Peace comes to us in times of grief when we have suffered the loss of someone very dear to us. Though the tears fall and the loss seems overwhelming, a deep sense of peace and comfort are also available to our hearts.

Peace comes to us in moments of crisis. Suddenly we are facing surgery or an unexpected bill we cannot pay or the loss of a job. Fear grips us, but God's peace overrides the fear and enables us to move on by faith.

No matter what the situation, God's peace is available and constant. It becomes our anchor in the storm, our security in the midst of uncertainty. When everything else fails us, His peace reigns in our hearts.

Extrasensory perception may serve a select few who find it comforting; but it is only one more of this world's substitutes. Christ gives us peace—true peace, His peace, peace that passes all explanations, peace that gives us calm, even while the storm is raging.

I marvel at the number of people who will call a hotline to hear some unknown person offer encouragement for the future. They're in search of something and they just do not know what God has to offer.

The real plan of peace rests solely in our Lord. Regardless of the circumstance, God speaks peace.

The "Super" Syndrome

For it is by grace you have been saved, through faith—
and this not from yourselves,
it is the gift of God—not by works, so that no one can boast.
EPHESIANS 2:8–9

One of the best stories I've heard recently concerns the former heavyweight boxing champion of the world, Muhammad Ali. It seems he was on a flight one day when the attendant said, "Please fasten your seat belt."

"Seat belt?" Ali replied. "Superman don't need no seat belt!"

And the attendant's reply was priceless. "Superman don't need no airplane! Now, please, buckle up!"

Our friend, Ali, is not the only one suffering from a superman or superwoman complex. Many of us have the urge to step into the nearest phone booth and come out with cape flying!

Some feel the pressure to be "Supermom." You know, work eight hours, fix the meals, do the laundry, spend quality time with the kids, serve on the PTA, and then be ready for bowling and pizza with the husband. Supermoms never tire, never get depressed, and they never, under any circumstances, get sick!

Then there is "Superdad." You might recognize him. He puts in seventy hours a week so that his family can have all the good things they deserve. He heads up the Scout troop and coaches Little League on Wednesday afternoons. He has the best manicured lawn in the neighborhood. He keeps both cars clean. He leads family worship, takes his wife on a date once a week, never sounds grouchy, and never watches Monday night football (as least not in its entirety!).

Know anybody who does all those things? Neither do I. But I know plenty who think they should and even more who keep trying. Why? Because we are performance-oriented. We find our worth in what we do, the degrees we earn, the awards bestowed upon us or our children, and the services we render.

It is no surprise that we carry that behavior into our Christian life. We strive to be "supersaints." We serve on several church boards, sing in the choir, lead a Bible study, spend at least three nights at the church, and we never, never, say no when asked to do one thing more.

Face it, none of us are supersaints! God never intended us to be. We didn't earn our salvation, and no amount of works will make us holy. Salvation is a gift offered us by a loving Father. He has already paid the price, and the gift is offered free of charge. We are not accepted by God for all of the good we do; we are accepted on the merit of Christ's work on the cross.

God doesn't love us more if we do more—He loves us even if we can't do anything! His love is truly unconditional and our significance grows out of that love.

We will make mistakes. We will fail. We will miss the mark, and we will need to ask for forgiveness more than once on many issues.

Forget about being a supersaint. Celebrate your uniqueness. Be the person God intended you to be, and rest in the storehouse of love that will not let you go.

A Different Measuring Stick

*"Whoever wants to become great among you must be your servant,
and whoever wants to be first must be slave of all."*
MARK 10:43

What constitutes greatness? In a world dominated by material-ism, we tend to equate greatness with possessions, wealth, and power. Yet in the Old Testament, a man's importance was mea-sured by how many cattle, sheep, and other animals he owned (remember Job?).

Are the cars in the driveway, the number of suits or dresses in the closet, the accumulation of electronic gadgets, or the titles on our door a measure of greatness?

When we think of "great" people, we tend to think of interna-tional leaders, super jocks, movie actors, or rock singers. We even dress like they dress, eat what they eat, and follow them around, waiting for an autograph or a glance in our direction.

It is not strange that the world would measure success this way, but I grow concerned when we allow that kind of mind-set to invade the church! When we do, we start thinking that the "great" pastors are the ones who have large congregations or television programs. We begin to think that big churches are better. Or we assume that those who write best-sellers and hit songs are the "suc-cessful" people in the kingdom.

Some are going to be blessed by God in these ways, but the material blessings do not equal success. We can pastor large churches, minister to huge audiences, sell a million books, and still fail miserably. All of that power and attention can turn even the most careful man or woman into a self-centered and self-reliant disaster. This is what happened to the Laodicean church described in Revelation 3:17.

Jesus measured greatness in terms of servanthood. That's what He tried to convey in the words recorded in Matthew 23 as well as in His daily life. Spiritual greatness is measured by humility, faithfulness, obedience, love, and many other qualities we tend to avoid. The Pharisees struggled with such a low-profile view of success, and we struggle too.

I have a dear friend whose wife of many years became confined to a wheelchair. A woman who had once cared tirelessly for him suddenly needed constant care herself. Totally unable to communicate with her, my friend simply served his wife day after day.

Such is "success" in the kingdom of God. No possessions accumulated on earth can take the place of love and service, of mercy and simple heartfelt commitment.

This is the "success" which truly matters.

Advent Eclipses Adversity

We are more than conquerors through him who loved us.
ROMANS 8:37

Adversity is a part of life. Sooner or later it knocks on all of our doors. Joseph and Mary were no exception. Their first Christmas was anything but festive and carefree.

Because of the uniqueness of Mary's conception, their reputations were in question. The young couple was faced with high taxes to pay. They were forced to make a trip they didn't want to make with the baby due any day. And to top it all off, there were no rooms in the motel for them. Even American Express couldn't help!

But that night, in a stable, something happened which made all of the adversities seem insignificant. A child was born—not just any child, but the Son of God! Mary became part of the miracle of Christmas! And adversity was eclipsed by joy. The story doesn't end there. The same power that transformed the journey of Joseph and Mary can transform our journey as well. And our world around us desperately needs to know this truth!

To all the wounded, grieving, hurting, lonely, helpless, and hopeless people around us, God is announcing the good news: *ADVENT ECLIPSES ADVERSITY!*

Christ is greater than any need we are facing. His grace is sufficient. His love is unending. His presence prevails.

People need to know this great truth about the gospel. People need to see this reality demonstrated in our lives. They need to know that Christianity is much more than a "prosperity gospel" in which everybody has plenty of everything that is desired materially or physically. They need to know Christ.

God never promises adversity-free living. I have never known a mature Christian who has not gone through adversity. Over the years I have watched dear saints deal with the worst that life can throw at us and, in the midst of the battles, demonstrate the grace of God.

We will experience tough times financially. We will suffer loss. We will not all "get well." We will not all be "delivered" from our problems. But we *will* become monuments to the power of God. We *will* prove that God is faithful and His Word is true.

To all of you who face adversity, take heart in the message that was born with the Savior: Advent eclipses adversity!

Flying Lessons

*To him who is able to keep you from falling and to
present you before his glorious presence
without fault . . . be glory, majesty, power and authority, through
Jesus Christ our Lord . . . now and forevermore!*
JUDE 24–25

I received a letter one day from one of the young families in our church. In it they shared some of the recent battles they had been facing. And as I read the letter I expected it to be signed by Job! Murphy's Law was indeed in effect—everything that could go wrong had gone wrong!

This father described physical pain, loss from fire, problems in the business, and substantial financial loss. Yet through all of these bitter experiences, this family had maintained their faith and were trusting God for the future. They were indeed holding on to faith, even in the midst of the refining.

One portion of the letter spoke volumes to me about God's abundant grace in our times of trouble.

"When Brooke, our oldest, was little, I used to throw her up in the air and catch her to squeals of 'more!' and 'higher!' After Daniel was born, I started doing the same to him. He, too, seemed to find pleasure in the game.

"Brooke, when three years old, saw me playing the game with Daniel, and she wanted to be thrown too. But when I threw her up as I'd done so many times, she was afraid. She set rules for how high and how fast. She was no longer sure this game was safe. She trusted her head more than her daddy.

"How much this is like the way we trust God. Sometimes He plays rough, and we don't like it. But He has a purpose for throwing us in the air. He wants us to learn to simply trust Him. He's teaching us to fly!"

Perhaps the trials in your life are flying lessons! Though you might feel unprepared for the game, perhaps God is growing your faith. And perhaps, if you listen close enough, you can hear the voice of the Father saying, "Trust Me! I won't let you fall!"

Peter's message has become a source of comfort to most of us who are familiar with pain. He wrote to folks who were under attack and enduring intense persecution. Here is his wise counsel:

Therefore, since Christ suffered in His body, arm yourselves also with the same attitude, because he who has suffered in his body is done with sin. As a result, he does not live the rest of his earthly life for evil human desires, but rather for the will of God. (1 Pet. 4:1-2)

Learning to fly is never easy. After all, we didn't come equipped with wings, and we certainly feel afraid when tossed high into the air.

But as we learn to trust Him, we discover that we've been safe all along. The Lord will not let us fall. Instead, He is teaching us to soar like the eagles.

When Nothing Happens

Therefore, my dear brothers, stand firm. Let nothing move you.
Always give yourselves fully to the work of the Lord,
because you know that your labor in the Lord is not in vain.
1 CORINTHIANS 15:58

We are so hung up on success in this country that we tend to measure everything in terms of results. If the bottom line doesn't show a profit, heads will roll. Should the team have a losing season, the coach is likely to be replaced. We give awards to those who finish first. Promotions go to those who make the most sales. Coupled with our drive to succeed is the desire to let everyone know how successful we are. So "success symbols" become very important. The big house by the lake, the designer clothes, and the expensive foreign car in the driveway say to all who go by, "I am successful."

Using that logic, most of us aren't very successful! A modest home in the suburbs, clothes from J.C. Penney's and an Escort in the driveway just don't cut it!

If we aren't careful this "he who gets the most results is the most successful" syndrome will creep into the church and our Christian lives. Then the pastor of the fast growing mega-church is more successful than the faithful shepherd of the small, rural congregation. We find ourselves bragging about how many "really sharp" people come to our church. In short, we adopt the world's value system.

A study of Scripture will reveal that results are not always immediate. The truth is, one can walk faithfully with the Lord, obey His Word, witness consistently and see very few results—at least no visible results. I was reminded of that recently in an article by Steve

Brown in which he related a story from his preacher friend Ben Haden. It seems he had preached a sermon where he felt the power of God in great abundance. The Spirit was at work. And yet when the invitation was given no one responded. He felt greatly distressed. The host pastor, noticing his disappointment, said, "Don't forget the parking lot." He looked out the window to see a young lady kneeling there praying to receive Christ as Savior. The lesson he drew from that was: We don't always have a window to see the parking lot.

Remember that the next time you get discouraged over seeing so few results for your labors and you're tempted to become weary in well doing. Results are God's responsibility, not ours, and He doesn't always work on our time schedule! Nothing we do for Him is ever done in vain. So keep on praying for those who need the Lord, be faithful in teaching your class, continue with family devotions, give your tithe, serve where the Lord has gifted you to serve—and leave the results to Him. And occasionally God may provide a window and allow you to see the parking lot. But even if He doesn't, results are taking place, and someday from the perspective of eternity we will learn just how "successful" we really were!

Gloria Gaither says it so beautifully:

Should the harvest never come, I will praise You;
Should I not tie the sheaves with my own hand,
I still will praise You for the promise of the sowing.
And though I should never see it, I know the harvest will be grand.

Should the harvest never come, I will not doubt You;
With joy I'll do the work that You have given me.
The seeds I plant are from the fruit of someone else's labor -
So I know there'll be a harvest that I may not ever see.

The God Who Restores

Restore us to yourself, O LORD, that we may return!
LAMENTATIONS 5:21

God reveals His truth to us in unusual places. For the prophet Jeremiah, the location was the potter's house. God simply said to Jeremiah, "Go down to the potter's house, and there I will give you my message" (Jer. 18:2). I have often wished God would say to me, "Dave, go out to the golf course and there I will give you a message for next Sunday." I keep listening intently for such a word but so far, nothing!

Upon receiving this instruction from God, Jeremiah did what we all must do if we want to discover more of God's truth—he followed His instructions. Revelation follows obedience! I don't know what the prophet expected to find when he got there, but what awaited him was a very common occurrence—or at least it appeared so at first sight. The pot this craftsman was working on was marred. Nothing unusual about that. Now comes the message. Jeremiah must have sensed God saying, "Watch what happens to the marred vessel; there is a valuable truth here I want you to learn."

Did the potter take the clay off the wheel and throw it in the trash in disgust? No. Did he fume, "I wish I had never made you; you're such a disappointment to me"? No again. He did what skilled potters do: He "formed it into another pot, shaping it as seemed best to him" (18:4).

God was using the potter to communicate to Jeremiah the glorious truth that His grace can restore that which has become marred by sin. We are a fallen race. According to Scripture we have all sinned and come short of God's glory. We are marred and only the Master Potter can repair the damage.

What does that holy, pure, and righteous God do when He sees our sinfulness and our failures? Cast us aside? No. Does He say, "You messed up, now there's no hope for you"? Never! His response was to send His Son to die on a cross for us! In Christ there is forgiveness, restoration, and healing. That is the good news of the gospel!

Sometimes even those who have experienced His grace and attempt to walk in obedience to His Word fail. We become marred. Others notice and want to write us off. God never does! His grace is like the rabbit in the commercial with the long-lasting battery inside—it just keeps going and going and . . .

The church is not a select club for perfect people. It is a gathering place for sinners saved by grace who love each other, minister to each other, and support each other—even when one of them gets marred. We are never more like the Father than when we are in the business of restoring those who have fallen. Remember, what sin has destroyed, grace can restore!

Remembering

*Remember the wonders he has done, his miracles,
and the judgments he pronounced.*
PSALM 105:5

A son went to visit his mother in the nursing home. Fearful that she might not recognize him, he stood at the foot of her bed and said, "Mother, what's my name?" She looked at him for a moment and replied, "Just stand there a few minutes, son, it will come to you."

Do you forget things? Most of us do. Some seem to have better memories than others. A select few even have what we call photographic memories. What a blessing—I think.

Actually, there are some things we ought to forget. The apostle Paul reflected on his life before he met Christ and it was not a pretty picture. Dwelling on some of his past experiences could have robbed him of his present joy and discouraged him from the ministry to which God had called him. That is why he declared, "Forgetting what is behind . . . I press on" (Phil. 3:13–14). Good advice! While we cannot totally block out the past, we can refuse to live there allowing it to zap our energy and destroy our peace. We can choose rather to focus on what God is doing and will do for us. A speaker at our church gave some wise counsel I have never forgotten: Don't keep looking in the rearview mirror.

There are other things, however, that we should never forget. The experiences of life teach us valuable lessons we need to pass along. God may meet a need in answer to prayer today that can strengthen our faith tomorrow. He puts special people in our lives who encourage and bless us, and remembering them can get us through some tough times. In Psalm 103:2 David says, "Praise the LORD, O my soul, and forget not all his benefits." He goes on to list some of them: forgiveness, physical healing, deliverance, love, compassion. We, too, need to write songs of praise to the Father as we remember all of His kindnesses to us.

Some of us make daily lists of "Things to Do Today." Why not compile a similar list called "Things to Remember Today." It might include such things as:

- Remembering to hug your mate and the other members of your family as you verbalize your love for them.
- Remembering to spend time in God's presence.
- Remembering to speak words of appreciation to those who make meaningful contributions to your life.
- Remembering to thank God for all His blessings.

Do it right now—before you forget!

Regular Customers

How great is the love the Father has lavished on us,
that we should be called children of God!
1 JOHN 3:1A

Years ago there was a professor named Pat McConnell who taught at Boston College. He was a favorite among the students who had come to value his keen insight and sharp wit. They were saddened to hear of his wife's death and wondered how he would react. At the first chapel service following his wife's funeral Professor McConnell began talking about his automobile that was now fifteen years old. It needed constant attention and often broke down, necessitating a call for help.

He explained that he was a regular customer at a certain garage, and the mechanic there always took care of him promptly, towing him in whenever needed. Even if there was a new Cadillac in the shop, it had to wait until Professor McConnell's car was attended to.

After telling that story, he closed by saying, "Fellows, I just wanted to say that God doesn't let His regular customers down either."

Good story, great theology! The Heavenly Father is consistently attentive and forever faithful to those who put their trust in Him and could be classified as "regular customers." The psalmist proclaims the faithfulness of God in Psalm 117.

Praise the Lord, all you nations;
extol him, all you peoples.
For great is his love toward us,
and the faithfulness of the LORD endures forever.

Jesus, in whom we saw a revelation of the Father, was the personification of compassion. He cared about people—all kinds of people. No one was unimportant. Everyone mattered. And He was always available!

While His love is extended to all, His all-sufficient grace is reserved for those who trust Him as Savior and walk in intimate fellowship with Him—the "regular customers." The tragedies of life come to all of us. Sickness, loss, heartache, disappointment, and death eventually visit all of our homes. For those who know the Lord there is the certainty of His grace and peace in the midst of the storm. After the most severe trial we are enabled to say, "God doesn't let His regular customers down." Are you a regular customer?

Letting Go of the Past

"Forget the former things; do not dwell on the past.
See, I am doing a new thing!"
ISAIAH 43:18–19A

A French youth watched as two Englishmen disembarked at the port of Calais. Before they knew what was happening, the young man had pushed them off the pier into the water. The two angry Englishmen climbed back onto the pier and demanded to know why this young man had pushed them in. "Is this any way to greet us as visitors to your country? Why would you do such a thing?" The young man replied, "That's for burning Joan of Arc at the stake!" "But that happened 500 years ago!" was the astonished response. "Yeah, I know, but I just heard about it this morning."

Some folks have a real difficult time letting go of the past! And, frankly, it is not always easy, especially when the past has been filled with abuse and unhappiness. Those who have been victims of sexual abuse, for example, often have to go through extended counseling before the past pain can be dealt with effectively.

My wife, who is chaplain at a local nursing home, shared a moving story with me recently. She has a sing-along for the residents there on a regular basis. They love to sing the old songs, including hymns. After a recent sing, one of the residents who is ninety-five asked Wanda if they could talk. Once in her room, this lady began to weep. It seems that when she was in the third grade her teacher insisted that everyone sing. When she did sing, however the teacher said, "That is terrible, don't ever sing again." She never did. And now, at ninety-five, she still lives with that rejec-

tion and has missed the joy of singing. That not only says something about the incredible power of words, but demonstrates how
difficult it is to let go of past pain.

There is no quick fix for releasing the hurt of the past; no verse
to quote that will instantly make it all go away. But God's grace is
sufficient, and as we give the pain to Him healing will come. He
bids us to cast all our cares upon Him because He cares for us.

The Holy Spirit is here as our Counselor, our Comforter, our
Cleanser. Give the pain to Him. The past cannot be erased, but He
can give you overcoming grace and set you free!

When Jesus is Jim

*We are therefore Christ's ambassadors,
as though God were making his appeal through us.*
2 CORINTHIANS 5:20A

There is a story that comes out of a Bowery Mission. It was at this mission that an alcoholic named Jim found Christ as Savior and sobered up to enjoy a brand new way of life. He eventually became part of the staff at the mission.

One night another man, as drunk as one can get, staggered into the mission. When they gave the invitation that night, he came forward and knelt. The counselor said, "Have you come to receive Christ?" The man looked up, "Is Jesus as good as Jim?" The counselor answered, "Yes, He's the one who made Jim good."

With that the fellow prayed, "I just ask that Jesus would take over my life and make me as good as Jim."

That reminded me of a pastor I knew in Ohio. He was sharing how he came to know the Lord, and said his journey began when he was dating a girl who attended one of our congregations in that city. A family there (we'll call the Jones family) took a real interest in him. They didn't preach to him, but they loved him and spent a great deal of time developing a friendship. One night as the service ended, this young man went to the altar to pray. When the pastor asked him what he needed, he said, "I want what the Joneses have."

Does anybody want what you and I have? Is there something about our lives that communicates the love of Christ? Do others see a peace and joy that is missing in their own lives?

64

Our job is not to try to attract people to us and our "goodness," but they do need to see Christ in us! Jesus said that our good works should bring glory to the Father. In other words, when we radiate Christ's love and our lives reflect the difference that only He can make, people will take notice. They will ask questions. And that gives us the opportunity to share the Lord with them and explain that we have no goodness of our own; it is Christ who has changed us.

Wouldn't it be great if someone knelt at your altar next Sunday and said, "I want what (your name) has."

Recycled Saints

*For he has rescued us from the dominion of darkness and
brought us into the kingdom of the Son he loves,
in whom we have redemption, the forgiveness of sins.*
COLOSSIANS 1:13–14

A local hospital has placed containers throughout the building
for the purpose of collecting aluminum pop cans. On the side of
the containers is the catchy slogan "Be a saint, recycle."

While recycling hardly qualifies one for sainthood, there is a
gem of biblical truth contained in that slogan. The fact is, all of us
who call ourselves Christians are recycled sinners who have been
changed by the grace of God. When God wanted to show
Jeremiah the extent of His grace for Israel, He had him go down
to the potter's house and observe him at work. As he watched this
skilled craftsman at his wheel, the pot he was working with
became marred. The potter simply reshaped it into a vessel of
which he could be proud.

All of us are marred by sin. Scripture is clear at that point—
there is none righteous, not even one! The sinful nature left
untreated disfigures us spiritually. We bear the emotional and
sometimes physical scars of living for the wrong values and serving
the wrong master. Some have been so enslaved to the power of sin
that any hope of restoration is dashed.

Yet the apostle Paul tells us in Romans that where sin abound-
ed grace does much more abound! God can take the worst sinner
and recycle his or her life into a thing of beauty! If any person is in
Christ, that person is a new creation (see 2 Cor. 5:17).

Here's the "rest of the story." Once we have been forgiven—recycled, if you will—we become part of God's recycling ministry. He sends us out to touch the lost and hurting, to bring them hope as we share with them the wonderful changes that Christ has wrought in our lives.

So there is great validity to the statement "Be a saint, recycle." That's what the church is all about! Next time you drink a can of pop be sure to place the empty can in an appropriate container. Next time you see a life that is marred by sin, let it be a reminder of God's transforming grace and an incentive to share His love with that person.

Commitment is a Process

"But your hearts must be fully committed to the LORD our God, to live by his decrees and obey his commands, as at this time."
1 KINGS 8:61

". . . for better or for worse, for richer or for poorer, in sickness and in health, for as long as we both shall live." I have performed scores of weddings over these thirty-seven years of ministry and have attended many more as a guest. Every time I hear the bride and groom repeating their vows I say to myself, "You have no idea what you are saying!"

I am not suggesting they are not sincere, only that they have no way of comprehending what those vows mean. It is relatively easy to promise to be faithful during times of sickness, and it may be if the illness turns out to be the twenty-four-hour flu. But what if it is an accident that puts the other person in a wheelchair for the rest of his or her life?

When we stand at the altar and say "for better or for worse" we are convinced it will all be for the better, but the truth is the storms will come, and most couples face times of intense testing. I have seen the death of a child or financial failure destroy marriages.

The point is, commitment is a process. Each new day will test our love for each other and the depth of our commitment to be faithful no matter what. Commitment always requires sacrifice and marriage is no exception. But for those who make the investment comes the reward of a loving relationship. The trials we face together can draw us closer to each other and strengthen the marriage. At that point the vows we made at the altar take on far greater meaning.

It strikes me that the same thing is true of our relationship to Jesus Christ. When we ask His forgiveness and begin a new walk of faith, we have no idea what will be involved. Our commitment to the Lord is sincere, but like the wedding vows, it has to be demonstrated over the ensuing years. We soon discover that the Christian life is not all mountaintops; there are valleys as well. There are those times when we have to walk by faith and not by sight. Times when our prayers don't seem to go any higher than the ceiling. Times when we ask "Why?"

James tells us we are to rejoice when the times of testing come because they enable us to develop perseverance and purify our faith. The end result is a deepening of our relationship with Christ.

Whether in marriage or the Christian life, commitment is a process. Unless we understand that truth, the failure rate will continue to escalate.

Secondhand Sin

Set an example for the believers in speech, in life,
in love, in faith and in purity.
1 TIMOTHY 4:12B

There is a controversy brewing presently over the effects of secondhand smoke. New medical findings are suggesting that great harm is done by breathing smoke being exhaled by smokers. One source says more than 53,000 non-smokers die each year as a result of secondhand smoke.

The tobacco industry, on the other hand, is saying that the tests that have been conducted are flawed and there is no conclusive evidence that secondhand smoke is harmful to non-smokers. An argument you would expect from people who make millions selling tobacco products.

The only proof I need is to be put in a room with smokers! I can't wait to find the nearest exit. There is no way the smoke I am being forced to inhale is not harming me! But my purpose is not to elaborate on the dangers of secondhand smoke. The point I would really like to make is that *many* of the things we do indirectly affect other people.

The children growing up in our homes are profoundly influenced by our actions and attitudes. If we exhibit strong prejudices, they are likely to follow suit. If we criticize the pastor around the dinner table, they may well form negative opinions of the church.

Certainly our moral and spiritual standards impact both our children and our peers. Abusive parents tend to produce abusive children. Moral permissiveness creates an atmosphere conducive to immorality.

Face it, the things our children see us reading and watching and putting our stamp of approval on will help to shape their value systems in the future. The Bible speaks of the sins of the parents being visited upon their children. We are seeing that happen at an ever-increasing rate of speed. Secondhand sin is just as destructive as secondhand smoke!

There is not yet a cure for cancer caused by smoking, but thankfully God has provided a cure for sin! Calvary is the cure! So by whatever means sin has come into your life, it can be removed. Secondhand religion isn't much better than secondhand smoke—be sure you have a personal relationship with Jesus Christ!

A Child Shall Lead Them

*"I tell you the truth, unless you change and become
like little children, you will never enter the kingdom of heaven.
Therefore, whoever humbles himself like
this child is the greatest in the kingdom of heaven."*
MATTHEW 18:3–4

Art Linkletter added to his popularity and made a ton of money by interviewing kids on TV. He knew a good thing when he saw it! Kids are totally honest—they just tell it like it is. I can recall programs where family secrets were divulged to the embarrassment of all concerned.

Moral: Don't ask a child a question if you don't want an honest answer. Sometimes they are not answering questions but just commenting on a situation, but the result is equally humorous. For instance, at my sixtieth birthday party one little guy was there with his parents. I was opening a large stack of funny cards when he spoke up and said, "You're so old you don't even get money in your cards!" Everyone laughed, but no one took up an offering!

I recall going up to a young child in one of the churches we pastored and telling him I had missed him lately. "Oh," he replied, "I've been in the hospital. I had my independence out." He meant his appendix of course, but the more I thought about what he said the more I realized that is an operation we all need to have!

There is a sense in which we all need to learn to be independent. Parents expect the day will come when their children leave home, get a job, assume responsibility for their future, and get on with their lives. A certain amount of self-sufficiency is commendable and to be encouraged. Even at the spiritual level we want to see new converts grow and mature to the point that they are not dependent on another person for their spiritual well-being, developing the disciplines of prayer and Bible study which lead to spiritual maturity.

But there is another sense in which we are to give up our independence. In fact, that is how we get into the kingdom of God in the first place. Jesus said "Blessed are the poor in spirit" [the spiritually bankrupt] (Matt. 5:3). They know they cannot save themselves so they call upon the grace of God.

That sense of total dependence on God's grace is to continue all through the journey that leads to heaven. Paul reminds us we can do all things through Christ—but only through Christ. He was an apostle with apostolic gifts and impacted the kingdom of God like perhaps no other person before or after him. Yet he confessed that he was in no way sufficient in and of himself. His sufficiency was of God! So is ours!

A Dream Revisited

Commit to the LORD whatever you do, and your plans will succeed.
PROVERBS 16:3

My wife was cleaning out desk drawers the other day and came across a couple of items she thought I might want to keep. One was a paper I wrote in high school with the caption "My Secret Ambition." My handwriting was as bad then as it is now, but I did manage to decipher it. My secret ambition was to be an evangelist. I wanted to travel all over the country and preach.

Part of the ambition was to find a wife who would share my dream and travel with me. I knew I probably couldn't do that forever, so I said that when I got old—about thirty!—I would settle down in a church and raise a family. We both had a good laugh when we read that line!

My ambition was sparked by the fact that I was a new Christian and a great admirer of Billy Graham. That admiration has never wavered over the years. What a genuine, humble servant of God!

Well, as it turns out, I didn't become an evangelist and travel over the country preaching. I did, however, find a wife who would put up with me and add immeasurably to my life and ministry, and if you ask her she probably would tell you we traveled across the country more than she would have liked to! Neither did I wait until the "old age" of thirty to accept a pastorate. I was barely into my twenties and as green as they come. People were constantly saying, "You don't look like a preacher." They don't say that anymore! I'm not sure if that's good news or bad news!

As I look back, I now realize the ambition was not abandoned, just altered by the One who charts our course. My ambition is still to preach His unchanging Word and to minister to those who need His touch.

What are your dreams and ambitions for the future? Do they include God? In a world that stresses self-gratification it is easy to live our lives for the wrong things. Jesus said the only way to find real happiness and real success is to seek first His kingdom and His righteousness. He is not against you succeeding in life—in fact, He wants the best for you. He just wants you to understand that life decisions made without Him can never produce lasting joy.

I didn't know which road God's will would take me down. I thought it was evangelism; it was pastoral ministry. But I did know I wanted to serve Him and that hasn't changed.

It's never too late—even if you're thirty!—to commit your ways to the Lord and seek His will for your life.

Trumpets and Bibles

How can a young man keep his way pure?
By living in accordance to your word.
PSALM 119:9

When I was in elementary school I wanted to play a musical instrument and be in the school orchestra. I told my teacher I would like to play the flute, but she said my lips were too big. (Since that time I have observed flute players with much bigger lips than mine, but as a sixth grader, I bought that explanation.) She suggested I play the trumpet. So I talked my parents into renting a trumpet from the school, and my musical career was launched.

Things were going pretty well, I thought, until one day after orchestra practice the director asked me if I had been practicing. I replied that I had indeed been practicing faithfully. She said, "Then how do you explain the fact that your trumpet has been here all week?" I had no answer.

From that point on my musical career took a downward turn. In retrospect I can now see that I wanted to *play* the trumpet but I didn't want to *practice*. Impossible!

Let me tell you what brought that childhood memory to mind. A few weeks ago my wife left her Bible at church. As I checked the information desk to see if it was there, I discovered a whole stack of Bibles waiting to be claimed. Wanda's was not in that collection. I remembered that there were also some Bibles on the rack next to the church office. Again, I was amazed at the number of unclaimed Bibles. Finally, I found Wanda's Bible on the pew where she left it. But I have thought a lot about all those other Bibles. Why haven't they been claimed? What if I were to go up to the owners and ask if they have been reading their Bibles? Would they give the same answer I gave my teacher?

In Paul's description of the armor of God in Ephesians 6, he mentions the "sword of the Spirit" (v. 17), which refers not to the Bible in general but to specific passages. In order to withstand the attacks of the enemy, we are to be able to quote chapter and verse as Jesus did in the wilderness. Every temptation of Satan was answered with a specific verse of Scripture that dealt with that issue.

You can't be a good trumpet player if you never practice. You can't be effective in spiritual warfare if you never study and memorize the Word. My guess is the Bibles left at church are not the only ones that aren't being read. Do you know where your Bible is? More importantly, are you reading it and committing it to memory?

Comforted to Comfort

And our hope for you is firm, because we know that just as you share in our sufferings, so also you share in our comfort.
2 CORINTHIANS 1:7

When God performs a work of grace in our lives it is seldom, if ever, an end in itself. When He extends forgiveness, for example, He wants us to share that message with others who need also to be forgiven and to forgive those who may have wronged us. When He prospers us, we are to share our blessing with those who have needs.

The same is true with comfort. Listen to what Paul writes in 2 Corinthians 1:3–4:

Praise be to the God and Father of our Lord Jesus Christ, the Father of *compassion* and the God of all *comfort*, who comforts us in all our troubles, *so that we can comfort* those in any trouble with the comfort we ourselves have received from God [emphasis mine].

I saw a perfect example of compassion this past Wednesday when the surgeon who did my wife's cancer surgery invited us to attend a cancer support group luncheon. There were several there who had experienced the removal of their bladders due to cancer. Each of them have visited and encouraged others who are facing the same surgery. One relatively young lady who had undergone this surgery said if it had not been for the visits of these former patients she could not have made it.

Most of them spoke also of a deep faith in God or revealed how this experience had brought them back to God. As I listened to their moving stories, my mind went back to Paul's words and I was more convinced than ever of the pressing need for support groups as a vital part of the church's ministry. There are so many hurting people who need comfort and understanding and encouragement. God has chosen to administer those things through us!

All of the people at the luncheon gave high praise to Dr. Elsaharty, and rightfully so; he is a man of great skill and deep compassion. He responded by saying, "You should be thanking God. Without Him I could not do this and you would not be alive." True, but God worked through a human being. He wants to work through you! Take a fresh look at all that God has done in your life and then ask Him to lead you to someone who needs what you have to share.

A View from the Motel

But encouraging one another daily, as long as it is called Today,
so that none of you may be hardened by sin's deceitfulness.
HEBREWS 3:13

I couldn't believe what I was hearing. It happened a few weeks ago when I was waiting in the lobby of a local motel for those who were joining me for a business breakfast. A gentleman, obviously from out of town, was asking the clerk at the front desk if there was a certain restaurant in our city.

The clerk replied that she was not sure but named a couple of other places where he could eat. At that point I spoke up and told him the restaurant he was looking for was right across the street. In fact, when you walk out the front door you can see it!

I find it incredulous that a person could work in a public place and not know what is across the street. But that is not an isolated case. When we moved to a pastorate in Cleveland, it took a long time to find our way around that city. Many times I would stop in a station and ask for directions and be told they had no idea where such and such a street was. I later discovered it was a block away from the station!

The truth is, most of us are not nearly as observant as we ought to be. Consequently, we miss many opportunities God sets before us to minister in His name.

Like the characters in the parable of the good Samaritan, we pass by on the other side failing to see the needs that God puts in our pathway. We ask how people feel, but we really don't want to know and we seldom listen when they actually try to tell us. Being insensitive to the Spirit, we fail to pick up on the moods of those around us. They may be hurting deeply, and the signals are there, but we miss them.

There are probably many opportunities every day to offer a helping hand, give a word of encouragement, provide a listening ear, or just be there for someone. Yet we are so preoccupied with our own agendas that it all goes unnoticed.

The more I think about the young woman at the front desk, the more I realize how much I am like her. I do know where that restaurant is—I like to eat there so I took the time to find it. But do I know where the hurts and needs and opportunities for service are? Can the Spirit direct me to these places or will He have to ask someone else?

Jesus was intensely aware of what was happening in the lives of those around Him. The Spirit will make us sensitive also if we allow Him to.

Back to the Basics

My son, keep my words and store up my commands within you.
Keep my commands and you will live;
guard my teachings as the apple of your eye. Bind them on your
fingers; write them on the tablet of your heart.

PROVERBS 7:1–3

Vince Lombardi, the legendary coach of the Green Bay Packers, was not pleased with the way his team was playing. He felt they were operating well beneath their potential. So he called a special team meeting and with unveiled sarcasm said, "Gentlemen, this is a football!"

He was making the point, of course, that they were going back to the basics and learning the game from the beginning. One of his players, who obviously didn't value his life, raised his hand and said, "Could you go over that again, Coach?"

It seems to me that it is high time that someone called our nation together and instructed them in the basics. We are rapidly becoming a valueless society. Even the highest court in our land has difficulty in defining pornography. There is a relativism abounding in our nation that defies absolutes and tears down any of the guidelines that protect a sense of morality and decency. It amazes me that the ACLU and other far-left organizations want to force upon America the very things that failed in the Soviet Union. We have drifted so far from the ideals and principles of our founding fathers, if they were to come back today, they would not believe they were in the same country.

The author of Proverbs declares that the "fear of the LORD is the beginning of wisdom" (9:10). Wisdom here means more than simply acquiring knowledge. When you study all of the facets of wisdom in Proverbs, you come away with what could be described as "a system of values." There is our answer! The basics we need to return to are the values God has taught us in His Word!

What's good for the nation in this regard is also good for the rest of us on an individual basis. Is your life guided by the values taught in the Scriptures? Is your family being built on this solid foundation? Or is society dictating your value system?

The church is not exempt. Far too often we have acquiesced to the pressures of a pagan world and tolerated values that are opposed to Scripture.

So perhaps it is time for the Coach to call national leaders, local and state leaders, educators, pastors, and heads of homes together and say, "Ladies and gentlemen, this is a Bible!" Someone will probably raise a hand and say, "Could you go over that one more time?"

Handfuls of Sand

*"Give, and it will be given to you. A good measure, pressed down,
shaken together and running over,
will be poured into your lap. For with the measure you use,
it will be measured to you."*

LUKE 6:38

Do you ever feel like what you're doing doesn't make a great deal of difference? I suppose we all have days like that. You know what I mean. You put forth a great deal of effort, you give it your best shot, and yet there is no measurable accomplishment. Maybe you can relate to the small boy I saw on the beach one morning. This little guy had undertaken a monumental assignment. He was attempting to take all of the sand from the beach and put it back in the gulf! He didn't even have a bucket and shovel—he was doing it two handfuls at a time!

I really admired his enthusiasm and dedication but I seriously doubt if there was any noticeable erosion of the beach when he finally retired for the day. Most of us have days when we feel like we've been trying to empty the beach one handful at a time; and maybe that's exactly what we've been doing! It is possible to give your best energies to things that really don't matter. But the feeling of wasted motion can also be very deceiving.

We live in a success-oriented society where we tend to measure everything in terms of tangible results. We reward the high achievers. But the truth is, great organizations, great institutions, great churches, and great companies are built in large means by those who carry the sand one handful at a time.

Jesus taught us that giving a cup of cold water in His name, visiting the sick and imprisoned, and ministering to the needy is of far more value than so many of the things we think are such big deals. He modeled for us the lasting value of servanthood. And servants don't always get a lot of glory. You don't always see what they are doing. They seldom make the headlines. At the end of a long day they sometimes feel about as "successful" as the little boy on the beach.

Just remember the next time you get weary in well-doing— when Satan is telling you what you're giving yourself to doesn't matter—that God's "well done" at the end of the journey is not for the over-achiever, the chairperson over everything, or the sought-after superstar. It is for the faithful servant who kept on giving when no one noticed and results were hard to define.

Hug Somebody Today!

All of you, live in harmony with one another;
be sympathetic, love as brothers, be compassionate and humble.
1 PETER 3:8

A man was headed for the county fair. He had a basket on his head, a pig under his arm, and a chicken in his hand. Being uncertain of the direction to the fair, he asked a lady who happened to pass by.

She told him to go one mile, turn left, go another mile turn left, and then go yet another mile and turn left once again.

The man said, "Wouldn't it be easier if we just cut straight through the woods?"

She replied, "No, if we did that you'd try to hug me."

"How on earth could I hug you! I've got a basket on my head, a pig under my arm, and a chicken in my hand."

"Well," she said, "you could put the chicken on the ground, cover it with the basket and I'll hold the pig!"

The lady obviously needed a hug! We all do. There is something affirming about a hug. It says "You're a nice person. I like you." You need to hug your husband or wife or children or parents every day—several times a day. You need to be alert during the day for people who need a hug to remind them they are valued as a person. My wife's ministry in the nursing home involves many different activities but one of the most meaningful things she does is to hug those dear people. It is a way to say, "I care about you."

Now I understand that some of you don't like to hug or be hugged. I am shy by nature and have to work at showing affection, so I can identify with you. A word of caution: We need to use discernment and good taste in hugging. I am not suggesting you run up to a member of the opposite sex and demonstrate your ability to give a bear hug! The biblical injunction to do everything in decency and order certainly applies to hugging. But everybody needs a hug, so find the folks God wants you to hug and make their day (and yours).

Tomorrow morning just sit quietly and meditate on God's love for you. Remember the length to which He was willing to go to forgive your sin and qualify you for heaven. Then picture Him wrapping His arms around you, giving you a warm hug, and saying, "I love you. You're important to Me. I care what happens to you today and I'll be there for you." Maybe that will make it easier for you to hug somebody in His name!

Childlike Faith

Jesus said, "Let the little children come to me, and do not hinder them, for the kingdom of heaven belongs to such as these."
MATTHEW 19:14

In the eighteenth chapter of Matthew we find the disciples asking Jesus, "Who is the greatest in the kingdom of heaven?" That subject came up often. Perhaps they secretly hoped that the Master would point to one of them and say, "You are!" What He actually did must have burst their bubble. He called a little child to Him and said, "I tell you the truth, unless you change and become like little children, you will never enter the kingdom of heaven" (v. 3).

The emphasis seems to be on humility—the willingness to admit we cannot save ourselves and becoming totally dependent on the grace of God. Actually there are many characteristics of little children we would do well to emulate. One of them is trust. Children place a tremendous amount of trust in their parents without even thinking about it. They trust them for protection, the necessities of life, an education, and a host of other things. Unfortunately, some parents destroy that trust and create lifelong emotional scars for their sons and daughters. But children by nature are trusting and sometimes display a simple faith we tend to lose as adults.

As I flew back from Florida where I had spoken at the Spiritual Emphasis Week for one our colleges, I observed several families traveling with small children. Again, the trust level of children became apparent.

The takeoff was a little bumpy and the seat belt sign stayed on the entire flight which doesn't thrill those of us who are not all that excited about flying to begin with. I have to admit that I seldom really relax on an airplane. But kids are different. As I walked to the rear of the plane I saw them engrossed in coloring books, playing games, laughing, enjoying the ride, and generally at ease. Some were even sleeping.

I ask myself why we don't have as much faith in our Heavenly Father as these little children have in an airplane. Maybe that's one of the things Jesus was trying to tell us.

Father, forgive me for putting more trust in the things that will pass away than I do in the One who changes not. Teach me to have a childlike faith that allows me to rest securely in Your love. *Amen.*

Spring Cleaning Theology

❦
〜〜〜⚮〜〜〜

"Woe to you, teachers of the law and Pharisees, you hypocrites!
You are like whitewashed tombs, which look beautiful
on the outside but on the inside are full of dead men's bones and
everything unclean. In the same way, on the outside
you appear to people as righteous but on the inside you are full
of hypocrisy and wickedness."
MATTHEW 23:27

Recently, on my day off my wife said, "It's time to start spring cleaning. Today let's wash all the woodwork, doors, etc." And I said, "Oh, boy, when can we start!" (Or something to that effect!) As we proceeded to clean I was instructed to move everything and clean in places nobody ever sees. To me that didn't seem like a good stewardship of time but Wanda explained to me why it was necessary. "It's like sin in people's lives," she said, "they clean up the areas people can see and then hide sin in their hearts."

By the time I had worked through all of the theological implications of that statement, we were finished cleaning (at least for the time being). My conclusion was that her illustration was right on target.

It is so easy for us to become like the Pharisees in our religious experience. You will recall that Jesus told them they cleaned up the outside but inwardly they were still a spiritual mess. (His mother probably made Him help with spring cleaning when He was a boy. Where else would He come up with a comparison like that?) These guys were long on rules and rituals. They loved elaborate ceremonies and took delight in putting their righteousness on display. But it was all show. They lacked a genuine experience with Jesus Christ that transformed them from the inside out.

I read in *Decision Magazine* the story of a woman who had been active in her church for fifty years—sang in the choir, served on countless boards, etc., and would have told you she was a "Christian." But then she went to a service at an evangelical church and the ladies who came to visit her explained how she could have a personal relationship with the Savior. That night she was born anew into the kingdom of God.

I'm afraid there are going to be a lot of folks greatly surprised at the judgment when God says, "Depart from Me, I never knew you." But they did so much good! They took part in so much "religious" stuff! Yes, but they never knew the cleansing power of the Cross; they never confessed their sinfulness and received Christ's forgiveness.

And what about Christians who hide "little sins" in their lives and refuse to deal with them? Those, too, will be revealed when we stand before the Father. The time to do spiritual house cleaning is now!

If you come to our house and move the furniture and check the baseboards, you will find they are clean. When the Spirit looks behind the surface areas of your life what does He see?

Take My Husband, Please

Search me, O God, and know my heart; test me and
know my anxious thoughts. See if there is any offensive way in me,
and lead me in the way everlasting.
PSALM 139:23–24

A well-dressed lady approached the pastor following the morning service. "I would like to make a donation to your overseas missions project," she said. Dollar signs began to register in the pastor's eyes as he anticipated the amount she had in mind. His heart sank as she added, "Would you take my husband?"

There are a number of ways to deal with difficulties in our relationships. One of them is simply to send the other party on a one-way trip to some foreign country. I don't recommend that approach. Another possibility would be to use the "deep freeze" method. You know, just don't speak to each other. Live in the same house but never communicate. That may be even worse than offering your mate for missionary service!

Other wrong approaches come to mind. For example, hold out until you get your way. Don't ever give in or admit you were wrong or, heaven forbid, ask forgiveness and assume part of the responsibility. And of course there is divorce. It's very easy now, and almost everybody's doing it.

May I suggest a much more constructive and satisfying answer. When you have conflicts, and we all do from time to time, begin by examining your own heart. Is your spirit right? Is the Father pleased with your attitude? Do you need to do some confessing and repenting? Are you being Christlike in your approach to the other person?

Now you are ready for some honest and loving communication. Nothing can be settled in anger, but a heart cleansed by the Spirit is ready to do whatever is necessary to bring healing and restoration.

Once you have cleared the air, pray with each other. Be honest. Tell God exactly how you feel and seek His help and healing.

Now take a close look at 1 Corinthians 13 and let that become the yardstick to measure your love for the other person involved. If both parties will do that and determine to apply the principles taught there to the relationship, neither of you will probably need to volunteer for missionary service.

Close Your Heads for Prayer

*So Eli told Samuel, "Go and lie down and if he calls you,
say, 'Speak, LORD, for your servant is listening.' "*
1 SAMUEL 3:9

When one gets up to speak on a regular basis, sooner or later the foot finds its way into the mouth. An incident from my first pastorate came to mind as I was sitting in our worship service recently.

I got up one Sunday morning to lead in the pastoral prayer, and I said to the congregation, "Let's close our heads and bow our eyes for prayer." Realizing immediately what I had said, I hurried right into the prayer hoping no one had noticed. To my great relief, no one said a word after the service. I was off the hook!

We sat down to our Sunday dinner only to be interrupted by a phone call. It was from one of my best friends at church who said, "Pastor, I just wanted you to know that before we ate dinner we bowed our eyes and closed our heads for prayer!"

We had several good laughs over that. One of the things you need to learn early on in ministry is to laugh at yourself. And believe me, I've had many opportunities to do so! But as I ponder that early blooper, it occurs to me that I may have spoken more truth than I realized at the time. There are probably too many times when we do "close our heads for prayer."

For instance, where are your thoughts during the pastoral prayer on Sunday? Are you entering in to the time of intercession or are you making plans for the day? Even in our own personal times of prayer it is so easy to ramble on and give God our shopping list for the day but never take time to *listen*. We give God no opportunity to speak to us because we perceive prayer as a one-way conversation.

Think about it for a moment. When you call your dearest friend to share what's going on in your life, do you say, "Hi, this is Jane" and then talk for thirty minutes, then say "good-bye" without ever giving your friend a chance to respond? Probably not. But we do that with God.

That, in effect, is closing our heads for prayer. In so doing we miss God's direction and insights the Spirit can impart to waiting hearts. So, today let's bow our heads for prayer and listen for the Father's response!

Invite Jesus to the Wedding

Now to him who is able to do immeasurably more than
all we ask or imagine, according to his power that is at work within
us, to him be glory . . . for ever and ever!
EPHESIANS 3:20–21

A Sunday School teacher was telling his class the story of Jesus attending the wedding at Cana where he turned the water into wine. When they had finished the lesson, he asked the class what they had learned. One little boy raised his hand and said, "If you're going to have a wedding, invite Jesus."

Right answer! Unless Jesus comes to our wedding and is made the third party in the relationship we call marriage, we are leaving out the one ingredient that can make it work in good times and in bad.

Forty-one years ago, on April 5, Wanda and I stood at the altar of the East Park Church of God in Dayton, Ohio, and vowed our love and faithfulness to each other for as long as we live. Like most couples getting married, we had no idea what those vows really meant. We were in many ways unprepared for the journey ahead. But we did one thing right. We invited Jesus to the wedding.

So many things have happened since that April day so long ago. College education. Two beautiful daughters. Seven extra-special grandchildren. Six pastorates. Financial struggles on a young pastor's salary. Uprooting family to follow God's call to another assignment. New and exciting adventures with the Lord that we never dreamed possible. Cancer. Heart disease. Lots of laughter. Lots of tears. Blessings. Burdens. Joys. Sorrows.

Has it been rewarding? Absolutely. Has it been easy? Certainly not! But we have learned some valuable lessons about marriage and life.

- God is greater than any problem we face and if we make Him our source we can survive every storm and grow closer together. God is faithful and His promises are true.
- The most important things in this world are the relationships we enjoy and the service we offer for Christ.
- Life's greatest joy is to give yourself away in ministry to people.
- Marriage takes commitment and work. There are constant adjustments and only those who really want to see it last will pay the price.
- Love gets better with age. If we were to repeat those vows again, they would have far more meaning than the first time!

I have been so blessed! God has given me far more than I deserve or ever expected. And when He gave me Wanda He outdid Himself! I wish for all of you who are entering into the wonderful relationship of marriage the same tough times, the same joys, the same commitment, and the same happiness. Be sure to invite Jesus to the wedding!

Don't Fix It!

The Lord . . . heals the brokenhearted and binds up their wounds.
PSALM 147:2–3

Most of us have heard the old saying, "If it ain't broke, don't fix it." Well, I want to give you a different version: "Even if it is broke, don't fix it."

I am not referring to appliances or automobiles. If your washer breaks down or your Chevy won't run, get them fixed. I'm talking about relationships and the hurts of life. For example, a friend comes to you devastated because her husband has just told her he wants a divorce. Or a grief-filled widow calls and tries to share her hurt through sobs and tears. What do you do?

Here's another scenario. You have been working with a teenager with serious problems. Everytime you think you're making progress the bottom falls out and you're back to square one. Or you've stayed close to a new convert and guided this person along on the journey of faith. He or she calls you one day and says, "I'm giving up my faith—I just can't make it." Click! End of conversation.

One more example. You're a parent who has done your best to bring your children up in a Christian home. You lived a consistent Christian life, you took them to church, had family prayer—all the right stuff. But they have not embraced the faith and are living apart from God. Now what?

These kinds of situations occur in all of our lives from time to time. When they do, we are tempted to be Mr. or Mrs. Fixit. The truth is, we can't fix broken hearts or broken lives. We can't live the Christian life for another. We can't fix broken marriages. God doesn't expect us to—that's His area of expertise. He told us to help bear one another burdens. That means being there with a listening ear. That means caring and praying and encouraging.

Only God can fix it! If we can remember that He is the Fixer and we are only the instruments through which He works, it can take a tremendous responsibility off our shoulders and free us to allow the Holy Spirit to work.

I wish I knew how to fix more things around the house. But I don't, so I call someone who does. There are so many lives I wish I could fix. But I can't, so I lift them up to the Father in prayer and do my best to be available as an agent of His grace. I am reminded of the sign in the mechanic's shop:

Charges: . . . . . *$10 an hour*
If you watch: . . *$15 an hour*
If you help: . . . *$20 an hour*

Lord, help me to remember that my job is not to fix people and their problems, but to point them to You. Help me to release them to the Holy Spirit and trust Him to work in their lives.

Amen

Determination

However, I consider my life worth nothing to me, if only I may fin-ish the race and complete the task the Lord Jesus has given me—the task of testifying to the gospel of God's grace.

ACTS 20:24

A young man made an appointment for an interview with a prestigious corporation. He asked if he could get into their well-respected training program. The very busy personnel manager, besieged by applications, said, "Impossible now. Come back in ten years." The applicant responded, "Would morning or afternoon be better?"

Determination—nothing is accomplished without it! It is not always the most brilliant or most gifted people who make it to the top of their profession; it is usually those who exhibit the most determination. Sometimes in a sporting event when the teams are fairly evenly matched, you will hear the announcer say something like, "Whoever wants it the most will win."

Determination is a factor in the Christian life also. We use the word *commitment* a lot, but what we often mean is determination. I have to make a decision to follow Christ and then determine that nothing will keep me from achieving that goal. Determination was one of the characteristics of our Lord while He was here on earth. Nothing could deter Him from His mission. He was determined to go to the cross and purchase our salvation.

I think of Nehemiah and the awesome task he was given. He had to somehow motivate people who had tried and failed before; he had to withstand relentless criticism and abuse in order to sort out the rubble and rebuild a wall which stretched out over some two and one-half miles. His secret: determination. He was doing what God had called him to do and he wasn't going to quit.

Few Christians have ever experienced the kind of hardships, persecutions, and rejection known to the apostle Paul. And yet, like Timex, he "took a licking and kept on ticking." He said, "I press on toward the goal" (Phil. 3:14). He was determined to faithfully carry out his calling and make it "home."

Some of the pioneers of our denomination whom I greatly admire knew the importance of determination. This old hymn by Charles Naylor and A. L. Byers says it well:

I mean to go right on until the crown is won;
I mean to fight the fight of faith 'till life on earth is done.
I'll never more turn back, defeat I shall not know,
For God will give me victory if onward I shall go.

How determined are you to serve Jesus?

How Does Your Garden Grow?

❦

Like newborn babies, crave pure spiritual milk, so that by it you may grow up in your salvation.
1 PETER 2:2

We were enjoying lunch with friends recently when the subject of gardening came up. Most of my experience with raising vegetables is past tense. I like the harvest but don't like weeding! My theory is Stokley does it better than I do, so I yield to their expertise.

Our friends have also decided that gardening is not high on their priority list. It seems their last garden didn't live up to expectations. Everything seemed to be going well—the seeds sprouted on time and grew into what looked like healthy plants. But when it was time to harvest the carrots, potatoes, and other vegetables, they were all very tiny in size. All of the growth had gone into the leaves and there was nothing under the soil!

The problem: The good soil was very shallow so there was no place for the plants to grow. It reminded me of the parable of the sower in Matthew 13:5–6. Of some seed Jesus said, "Some fell on rocky places, where it did not have much soil. It sprang up quickly, because *the soil was shallow.*" He goes on to point out that the seeds did not grow because *"they had no root"* [emphasis mine].

Some Christians look good on the surface. They know the right verses and serve on several boards and do all the right things. And then suddenly they are gone—no longer attending church, no longer serving. In fact, no longer professing to be believers. What happened? A lot of excuses are offered, but most of the time it is simply because they did not provide soil that allowed the Word to grow and produce fruit.

In order to make it, one has to first of all make a genuine commitment to crown Jesus Lord. After that come the necessary disciplines of prayer, Bible study, accountability, and witnessing. These are not options. Without them the seed will not grow.

If our friends ever attempt to get back into gardening the *first* thing they will do is check the soil to make sure it goes deep enough to allow for growth. If we are serious about growing in the Christian faith, we will be very careful to pull out the weeds of worldliness and carelessness so that the Word might take root, go deep, and yield a harvest of holiness from within.

Get Out of the Way

❦

*Trust in the LORD with all your heart and lean not on
your own understanding; in all your ways acknowledge him,
and he will make your paths straight.*
PROVERBS 3:5–6

The conductor Toscanini apologized to a symphony orchestra
once for losing his temper and yelling at them. He said, "The trouble is that God keeps telling me how the music is to be played, and
you—you keep getting in the way."

I think that is the way Jesus felt about the Scribes and Pharisees.
He kept teaching the good news of forgiveness and acceptance and
freedom, and they kept getting in the way with their endless list of
rules and rituals. The symphony of grace was being ruined by
legalists playing off-key.

So much for the Scribes and Pharisees. It's easy to pick on
them—they lived way back there! But what about you and me?
Do we ever get in the way of what God is trying to do? I don't
know about you, but I have to plead guilty.

I get in the way when . . .

I try to play God in other people's lives and don't trust them to
the Holy Spirit.

I lay out my plans and fail to spend time in prayer to see if this
is what God really wants.

Allow my sense of humor to get misplaced.

Say yes or no to an assignment or request without seeking God's
direction.

Does God get angry and yell at me like Mr. Toscanini? No, at least I have never heard Him do so. Fortunately, He is loving and patient and forgiving. But I think there are probably days when He says, "Dave, if only you would come to Me first I could save you a lot of grief and you wouldn't get in the way of the music."

There are times, however, when I find myself in harmony with His will and blending in with the divine symphony and it feels great!

Lord, show me the right notes to play and teach me when to come in and when to keep silent. I don't want to get in the way, but I will unless Your Spirit guides me. Give me ears to hear what He is saying to me.

Amen.

A Bouquet of Roses

Let your light shine before men, that they may see your good deeds
and praise your Father in heaven.
MATTHEW 5:16

Do you have trouble receiving a compliment? I do. I received one once and didn't know how to handle it. Seriously, most of us find it hard to know how to respond to compliments.

I read about an incident in the life of one of the great warriors of the faith, Corrie ten Boom, that will help all of us the next time somebody says "Great job!" or "You sang beautifully this morning!" or "Honey, that was a wonderful meal."

Someone asked Corrie how she handled all of the compliments and praise that were heaped constantly upon her without becoming proud. She said she looked at each compliment as a beautiful long-stemmed flower given to her. She smelled it for a moment and then put it in the vase with the others. Each night, just before retiring, she took the beautiful bouquet and handed it over to Jesus saying, "Thank you, Lord, for letting me smell the flowers; they all belong to You."

What a great idea. It was an act of humility which said: While I like myself and appreciate the affirmation of others, I recognize that I am what I am by the grace of God. The glory really belongs to Him.

I'm sure that Corrie also received her share of criticism—anybody who is doing anything usually does. I feel certain she took those to the Lord also. Not to say, "Here, this is Yours." but with the assurance that God shares *everything* that comes into our lives.

So, what do we do with compliments? We enjoy them, then thank the Lord that He works through us, and pass the bouquets along to Him. And when the criticisms come, we know that we can also go to Him and He will be there to share our hurt and to help us learn from them.

In thirty-seven years of ministry I have received more compliments than I am worthy of and probably more criticism than I deserved. I got credit for things I had little to do with and I got blamed for things I had no control over. As I look back it appears God has allowed a balance between the two to keep me from undue pride or depression.

Compliments and criticism—they are part of life. It's very wise and healing to share them both with the God who loves you unconditionally!

Home at Last!

But our citizenship is in heaven. And we eagerly await a Savior
from there, the Lord Jesus Christ.

PHILIPPIANS 3:20

Home at last! After six different flights, thousands of miles, seven different beds, countless restaurants, moving seven pieces of luggage many times, and preaching seventeen sermons we arrived back in Anderson. While we thoroughly enjoyed our ministry and the opportunity to visit with old friends, it was really good to get home.

I was reminded that the greatest title for heaven is probably "Home." We are all on a journey that will end with what we call death. But death is not the end—it is only the transition from this life to the next. And for those who know Christ as Savior, that will be a great homegoing time!

Like Abraham, we are strangers here looking for a city not made with human hands. As the old song says, "This world is not my home, I'm just a passin' through."

But one of these days we'll move from this "tent" to our eternal home. We can unpack and never have to move again! One of my friends in California loves to play practical jokes. When we got off the plane in Los Angeles (where we used to pastor) and came down the exit ramp, there was this big sign on one of the posts which read: WELCOME HOME, BROTHER DAVE! He had his video camera out, and everyone was staring at me wondering who in the world Brother Dave was!

When our journey here ends and we cross over to the other side, there will be One to greet us whose hands still bear the scars put there for our sin. I have a feeling He might say, "Welcome home, I've been expecting you."

For some of you that day may be a long way off, for others it may be very soon. But all of us will step from time into eternity someday. Will that be a homecoming day for you? Or will you hear the Savior say, "Sorry, I never knew you"? You are choosing your destination now. Jesus says He is the ONLY way to heaven.

Have you asked Him to forgive your sin and become your Savior? If so, one of these days you will look around and be able to say, "Home at last!"

Sound the Alarm

*But our citizenship is in heaven. And we eagerly await
a Savior from there, the Lord Jesus Christ.*
PHILIPPIANS 3:20

We spent a long weekend recently on the beautiful and historic Nantucket Island. It is like stepping back in time to walk through this town where many of the structures are over a hundred years old and the newer ones are designed to look like they came from the same era. The friends with whom we were visiting insisted that we see the Episcopal Church. We fully intended to do so, but it was our last night on the island and we still had not been there. On our way back to the room where we were staying we decided to take the time to go in and spend a few minutes in the sanctuary. The doors were unlocked and there were some dim lights which added to the quiet beauty of this ancient place of worship.

As we left the church and continued walking we suddenly heard a voice behind us saying, "How are you folks tonight?" We turned and to our surprise it was a policeman. We told him we were fine, and then came the second question: "Were you folks by any chance in the church a few minutes ago?" When we confirmed that we had been, he informed us that we had set off the silent alarm at headquarters!

I had visions of being locked up in a cell overnight. I could just hear my cell mate saying, "I'm in for armed robbery, what are you in for?" "Praying in the church!" How would this news be interpreted by my home congregation? Would the fact that my wife told the cop I was a preacher only add to my sentence?

My anxiety was misplaced. The officer was very friendly and told us to have a good evening. We had a good laugh over the whole incident, but as I pondered what had happened, several questions came to mind. For starters, why did the church leave the doors unlocked and then install an alarm system? More importantly, what does it take to set off an alarm in the church where I pastor? What has to happen before we are concerned enough to take action?

You may want to ask the same question about the place where you worship. Do alarms go off when we see our society drowning in a sea of immorality? Does the death of millions of unborn babies demand that we speak out and get involved? Will we allow the damaging teachings of secular humanism to go unchallenged? Can we view the homeless and not feel compassion? I repeat, what has to happen before alarms go off in our congregations that signal the time for action has come?

As it turned out, the alarm we set off in the church did not require any involvement from the police department beyond checking out the cause. The forces that are destroying our value systems, breaking up our families, and weakening our nation do demand response. The alarms are sounding. Do we hear them?

Running Out of Gum

A friend loves at all times, and a brother is born for adversity.
PROVERBS 17:17

What a pleasant surprise! My church mailbox was overflowing with cards from the children who participate in our children's choir program on Sunday night. Each child sent a personal message and attached a stick of gum. A week or so later I visited one of the young men in our congregation who was recovering from surgery. He, too, had gotten cards from the youthful choir members. His, of course, were get well cards and each of them was accompanied by a stick of gum. The one that got my attention said, "Get well soon, we're running out of gum!"

Leave it to kids to get right to the point! I had several good laughs over that card, but the more I thought about it, the more I realized that even as adults we sometimes adopt a similar attitude toward those in our midst who have needs. When sickness or death or a financial crisis hits, we are there doing all the right stuff . . . for awhile. Let the sickness linger for weeks or months and we tend to slack off in our attention. Once the funeral is over, we move on to other needs, forgetting that the worst days for those who are grieving lie before them. Immediate financial assistance is one thing, but the long-term support is quite another matter. In every instance we quickly run out of gum!

There are circumstances where short-term involvement is all that is required. But there are other times when people need us for the long haul. As previously mentioned, the pain of grief does not quickly leave us. The trauma of divorce lingers for months, even years. Finding emotional healing for the damage inflicted through sexual abuse requires long-term commitment on the part of the care-giver. Packs and packs of gum are needed!

The difference between saying we care about people and the willingness to get involved in their needs for as long as it takes to find solutions is commitment. It is relatively easy to send a card, take over a meal, or make a phone call. It is a lot tougher—and a thousand times more beneficial—to be there for that person when it costs us something in terms of sacrificing time and energy and saying in tangible ways, "I really do care about you, and I'm here for you."

Worth Waiting For

Wait for the LORD; be strong and take heart and wait for the LORD.
PSALM 27:14

We are an impatient people. Our theme song is, "Lord, give me what I ask for, and give it to me NOW." Our passion for instant everything has produced fast-food restaurants, supermarket express lines, an endless array of frozen dinners, and one-hour cleaners.

Unfortunately, this mind-set has carried over into the spiritual realm as well. One psychologist commented that his experience confirmed the fact that no one is willing to wait for anything anymore, not even those who call themselves Christians. They want God to make them happy without standing in a waiting line.

His evaluation is verified by the messages we often send up to God disguised as prayers. Things like, "Heal me, Lord, and do it today." "Save my marriage, God, and hurry because there isn't much time left." "Make our church grow, and make it happen quick because the congregation down the street is gaining on us." "I need to know Your will for my future . . . by sunup tomorrow."

Psalm 37 ought to be required reading for this impatient generation. David recommends several things in this psalm, none of which appeal to those looking for instant answers. He begins by saying, (1) "Do not fret" and immediately fouls up our game plan! He goes on to say, (2) "Trust in the LORD" which may, of course, require some delays. Then it gets even tougher: (3) "Commit your way to the LORD" which involves giving up control. And finally, (4) "Be still before the LORD and *wait patiently for him*" [emphasis mine].

God doesn't ask us to stop fretting, put our trust in Him, surrender to His will, and wait patiently before Him because He tires of hearing from us or enjoys watching us squirm. He knows that there are lessons we need to learn that will be missed if we do not listen to His still, small voice. The answers to our questions and requests are often enhanced by a waiting period during which the Spirit teaches us some valuable lessons. We cannot put God on a stopwatch. Once the request has been committed to Him, we need to trust His love and wisdom to do what is best for us over the long haul.

Just because God doesn't answer today is no indication that He has not heard or that He is denying the request. It only means He is working in ways that we cannot see. In His time the answer will come. Remember, the secret closet is not an express line—it is a waiting room!

Make Mine Vanilla!

There are different kinds of gifts, but the same Spirit.
There are different kinds of service, but the same Lord.
There are different kinds of working,
but the same God works all of them in all men.
1 CORINTHIANS 12:4–6

I have a very unique friend who lives on the West Coast. He is one of the neatest guys I have ever known. One of the things he used to love to do was get ice cream. We would drive any distance necessary to get to one of those ice cream stores where they have an endless list of flavors to choose from.

Without exception he would look over the list and then say, "Make mine vanilla!" Can you believe it! Why, with such flavors as rocky road, pecan, strawberry, and peach would someone order vanilla every time?

If I knew the answer to that question then I would also know why we do the exact same thing in so many other areas of our lives. For example, why do we come to church Sunday after Sunday for years and expect everything to be exactly the same? There are a variety of meaningful ways to worship God and express our praise (and no method is sacred!), but we have a tendency to say, "Make mine vanilla." Interpretation: Keep it the same as it has always been.

We could apply that same mind-set to all of the church's ministries. Don't change my Sunday School class, don't tamper with the Sunday night service, don't alter the format for Wednesday, etc. Why not? There are always new and creative ideas to explore and fresh ways to present the old, old story. Back comes the response: "But we've always done it this way!"

My point is not to suggest we change everything for the sake of change. That is never a worthy motive. Some things should never change! But methods, programs, and approaches need to be changed constantly to be in tune with the times. What worked twenty years ago may not work in the 1990s. The church that makes an impact on this pagan world for Christ is the church that stays on the cutting edge.

Have you noticed the pizza ads? The competition is tough, so pizza places must offer a wide variety to choose from. You can order pan pizza, hand-tossed pizza, or thin crust pizza. Select from a whole list of ingredients, and the possibilities are almost endless.

I cannot imagine going into a pizza restaurant and ordering a plain cheese pizza—every time—or going to the ice cream store and saying, "Make mine vanilla"—every time.

Nor can I imagine approaching the work of God with my mind set in concrete on how things need to be done. I want to be true to the Word, faithful to Christ, and uncompromising in my commitment to Him. But I also want to be open to any new direction the Spirit might want to take me; to any new methods that would reach more people with the gospel; to the creativity of the One who created all the variety we see around us.

A Dollar Well Spent

A wise man's heart guides his mouth,
and his lips promote instruction. Pleasant words are a honeycomb,
sweet to the soul and healing to the bones.
PROVERBS 16:23–24

"We can improve your communications for one dollar a day." That's what the lady from the phone company said. I had called to get the weather report and heard this unexpected good news. But before I invest my dollar I need to ask myself if this bargain is providing something I really need.

Do I need to improve my communication skills with the people I work with and meet every day? Yes! Like most people, I too often fail to give the words of encouragement others need to hear. And sometimes the words I do speak don't convey what I intend to say. Would you believe that a few times in my life I have actually been misunderstood! Sure, I'll pay a dollar to improve in this area of communication!

Do I need to improve my communication skills with my wife? Yes. We have a good, solid relationship for which I thank the Lord every morning, and we do communicate. But, like most husbands, I have room for improvement. I need to put into words more often what I feel in my heart. I need to say, "That was a great meal, honey" or "You look great in that outfit" or "I really appreciate the way you keep the house clean and iron my clothes." Does that put any of you others guys under conviction? Maybe we ought to invest a dollar and improve together! Perhaps they even offer a group rate!

Do I need to improve my communication skills in prayer? Most definitely. Prayer is my most important source of strength, wisdom, and inspiration. It is the single most important thing I do. I want my prayer life to be an ever-deepening relationship with the Father. I'm not especially concerned about knowing better words to use in my conversations with Him, because He understands what I need before I ask. I am interested in learning to communicate with Him in the truest sense of that word. A dollar would be a cheap price to pay for a more satisfying communion with God!

Do I need to improve my communication skills in preaching? Oh, yes! My deepest desire is to communicate faithfully the Word of God. A dollar would be a small price to pay in order to proclaim the good news more effectively. Maybe some of my members would chip in the buck!

A Word to the Diet Conscious

For physical training is of some value,
but godliness has value for all things, holding promise for both
the present life and the life to come.
1 TIMOTHY 4:8

Perhaps Americans have never been more health conscious than they are right now. It is difficult to pick up a magazine these days without reading an article on the hazards of cholesterol. Who ever thought oat bran would become so popular or that chicken would cost more than steak!

Low fat diets are in and so is exercise. Joggers are as common as cars and health spas have growing memberships. We are consuming foods reported to lower our risk of cancer and making sure we have enough fiber in our diet.

I suppose it is good that we are taking a more active role in maintaining good health, but I wonder if we are overlooking some areas that are equally as important as diet and exercise.

The writer of Proverbs said, "My son, do not forget my teaching, but keep my commands in your heart, for they will *prolong your life* many years and bring you prosperity" (3:1–2; emphasis mine). A little farther down in the same chapter we read, ". . . fear the LORD and shun evil. This will bring *health to your body* and *nourishment to your bones*" (3:7b–8; emphasis mine). Move to chapter 15 and hear this health-giving counsel: "A cheerful look brings *joy to the heart* and good news gives *health to the bones*"

(15:30; emphasis mine).

What we do to maintain the body is important; what we do to strengthen ourselves spiritually is of even greater value! A negative, critical, doubting, undisciplined spirit will destroy us no matter how big our muscles get! Diet is very important, but I am reminded of the words of Jesus, "What goes into a man's mouth does not make him 'unclean'" (Matt. 15:11). This He spoke concerning the Pharisees who were strict in their diet but spoke from hearts that were far from God. Their diet didn't make them holy and our diet won't make us healthy if in our hearts there is bitterness, resentment, or guilt.

Go to your doctor and get your cholesterol level checked, stay on a balanced diet, and get adequate exercise. But make sure you also feast on God's Word and consistently adhere to the disciplines of the faith that produce spiritual maturity.

Pretty Blue Umbrellas

Am I now trying to win the approval of men, or of God?
Or am I trying to please men?
If I were still trying to please men, I would not be
a servant of Christ.
GALATIANS 1:10

I had to make a decision. This was no time to straddle the fence. Here I was in the hospital parking lot ready to go in and make calls. Just before I got there it began to rain hard. I looked in the backseat for my black umbrella. It was not there! Then it dawned on me—I had put it in the other car.

Now comes the hard part. There is an umbrella in the car, but it is my wife's cute pastel blue model! Decision time! Do I go without the umbrella and get soaked or do I carry the light blue umbrella and run the risk of people staring at me? I made the macho choice and got wet! Of all days to wear light tan trousers!

Why did I do that? For the same reason we all make some of the choices we make each day—I was worried about what other people might think. Peer pressure is intimidating and we all yield occasionally. I feel for our young people at school. It has never been easy to go against the flow, but it has probably never been harder than it is today. We really need to support our youth in prayer. But they are not alone in dealing with peer pressure. It is just as real in the factory, the office, social gatherings, and almost everywhere we go.

Paul warned us in Romans not to allow ourselves to be pressed into the world's mold, but the pressure to do just that is relentless!

We are confronted everyday with values that are opposed to godliness. We are pressured to go along with the crowd and not make waves. No doubt about it, if you are determined to live the Christian life on a consistent basis, you will be a square peg in a round hole!

Let's be honest and admit that it is not easy to stand against the tide. What others think is important to us. But so is what our Heavenly Father thinks!

The bottom line is: What matters most to us—what other people think or what God thinks? We need a few more Daniels around who aren't ashamed to identify with a holy God and a few more Pauls who aren't ashamed of the gospel.

I'm going to pray for more courage to ignore what people think. And if you see me carrying a pretty blue umbrella, don't you dare laugh!

A Purse That Lasts Forever

*For what was glorious has no glory now in comparison with
the surpassing glory. And if what was fading away came with glory,
how much greater is the glory of that which lasts!*
2 CORINTHIANS 3:10–11

When the doctor restricted the amount of weight I could lift to forty pounds I knew there was one thing I could no longer do: carry my wife's purse! Like most women's purses, hers is a cosmetic center, drug store, hair styling salon, bank, and general storing area for hundreds of items. For that reason, and due to the fact that it gets so much use, Wanda's purses, like yours, wear out.

What do you have that doesn't wear out? Well, there are some rocks in the backyard that seem to be holding up pretty well, but, other than that, most items have their day and end up being put out on Friday for the trash collector. I don't have any secret formula to make things last but I do want to make you aware of a purse that never wears out.

Jesus spoke about it in Luke 12:33 when He said, "Provide purses for yourselves that will never wear out, a treasure in heaven that will not be exhausted, where no thief comes near and no moth destroys." That comes at the end of a discourse in which He tells us not to worry about the things that the pagans ran after—food, clothing, money, etc. All of those things, while necessary for life, are never to become obsessions and do not represent our source of security. They are, if you will, purses that wear out.

Life lived with eternal values as top priority, life full of faith and trust in God as Provider, and life given away in service and ministry represent a purse that never wears out. Come to think of it, everything God gives is underwritten with an unconditional, eternal guarantee! The Bible speaks of the "garment of praise." We can wear that forever—it will always be in fashion around the throne!

Jesus said He would give us His peace. The guarantee is that nothing in this world can take it away from us, and heaven will only increase its value. We have right now, in the midst of this dark world, a "blessed hope." It will shine brighter as it becomes a forever reality. Think of the fruit of the Spirit—will we cast those aside in heaven? No, because we will be in the presence of the One who is the personification of those qualities and we will be like Him!

Do you want to spend your life putting things in purses that constantly wear out, or would you prefer purses that last forever?

Jelly Beans and Temptation

For we do not have a high priest who is unable to sympathize
with our weaknesses, but we have one who has
been tempted in every way, just as we are—yet was without sin.
Let us then approach the throne of grace
with confidence, so that we may receive mercy and find grace
to help us in our time of need.
HEBREWS 4:15–16

Are you ever tempted? If you answered no, you probably are dishonest about other things too! Temptation is something we all deal with. It is one of Satan's oldest and best methods of bringing pain and destruction into our lives. It worked in the garden with Adam and Eve, and it still works.

The form of temptation will vary with each of us because we are all vulnerable in different areas. What tempts you may not affect me at all. Satan knows our weaknesses and that is one area he attacks. But he also knows our strengths and tries to seduce us there with pride and vanity. The "big head" has probably ruined as many Christians as lust! Maybe that's why Paul reminds us not to think more highly of ourselves than we ought to think.

Some temptations are almost impossible to avoid. We live in a media society. Therefore, we are subjected to all kinds of communication designed to squeeze us into the world's mold. The message is so incessant that if we aren't careful it wears us down and wins us over. Other temptations we can avoid if we want to. For example, I know if I have a bowl of jelly beans by my desk or a dish of mixed nuts anywhere in the same building, I'm going to eat them! So what should I do? Put several of each in front of me and say, "I will not eat these," or refuse to buy them and remove the temptation?

Maybe you can look at jelly beans all day and never eat even one. I can't! You say, "You're weak in that area." Right! You got my point! Now let's apply it to the Christian life. When you know something bothers you spiritually, stay as far from it as you can get. If there are certain people who drag you down with them, don't run with that crowd. If viewing certain things creates feelings of lust, stop looking at them.

God has promised us that with every temptation He will make a way of escape—but He also told us to resist the devil and shun the very appearance of evil. You wouldn't put your bed in the middle of the road and then blame God if a car hit you, would you? Then don't engage in things you know can hurt your walk with God and then wonder why you don't have any power to overcome temptation.

The Power is Back On!

*I want to know Christ and the power of his resurrection
and the fellowship of sharing in his sufferings,
becoming like him in his death, and so, somehow, to attain to
the resurrection from the dead.*

PHILIPPIANS 3:10

Twice in a period of three weeks our power went out. Once for twenty-four hours and once for nine hours. What a hassle! Our house is all electric so when the power goes off everything goes off!

We turned on the faucets but no water came out because our well pump runs on electricity.

We couldn't use our microwave or range because they both take electricity.

No light. No heat. No garage door opener. No way to keep food cold.

No way to wash your hands. No way to flush. No way to shave or shower.

Life is no fun with the power off!

Before Jesus came, there was no power for living. The human race was ravished by sin with no way to overcome the powers of darkness. Life's greatest tragedies had to be faced with no inner resources. The grave was the dreaded end to a life without hope and meaning.

THEN CAME THE CROSS AND EASTER!

THE POWER IS ON!

That's what we celebrate on Easter Sunday—and every Sunday! Christ defeated all of the powers of darkness and sin and robbed the grave of its victory! The Bible says the same Spirit that raised Jesus from the grave is now at work in us!

Trying to live without that Power is like trying to operate your home without electricity. Nothing works the way it should. There is nothing but frustration, anxiety, fear, and defeat.

Don't get me wrong, Easter doesn't remove the obstacles common to life. It did not remove sin from the world or make us free from temptation. But it did give us victory over all of these things—including the grave!

The Resurrection should not be something we celebrate once a year. We ought to get out of bed every morning and shout:

Hallelujah! Christ arose! Easter is a reality in my life! I am more than a conqueror through Him who loves me! Praise God, the power is back on in my life!

Voice Control

There is . . . a time to be silent, and a time to speak.
ECCLESIASTES 3:1,7

Why do we always feel we have to say something? Why is it that when a loved one or friend is told they have a terminal disease we have to burden them with trite cliches? Why is it when we go to the funeral home to express our love we feel it necessary to say a lot of words to people who cannot process a lot of words at that point?

The same question could be asked when we visit parents whose son as been diagnosed with AIDS, or a wife whose husband has just walked away with another woman. Why do we think we have to make everything right by trying to talk them out of their pain?

The Preacher wisely said, "There is a time to *be silent*" [emphasis mine]. Sometimes people just need a friend who will *be there*. Your very presence says you care. A grasp of the hand, a hug, or just sitting with them can do far more good than meaningless words.

I remember a dear man in one of the churches we pastored whose wife was dying with cancer. It had been a long and painful battle and it was nearing the end. She was in the hospital once again. I had been there in the afternoon and left for a wedding rehearsal. Following the rehearsal I returned to the hospital room. It was late evening now and most of the lights were out. Her room was dimly lit. As I recall, I came in, patted him on the shoulder, and sat down next to him. I stayed for an hour or two and left. We probably didn't speak twenty words the entire time. We didn't have to. I knew he was hurting too much to talk; he knew I loved him and hurt for him. There were no words to speak; none were necessary.

There is a time to be silent. There is also a time to speak. If we are sensitive, the Holy Spirit will give us the right words at the right time. Words, properly spoken, can bring healing and hope, and encouragement.

As I waited outside the surgery room all alone many thoughts raced through my mind. A young man, who I assume worked for the hospital, walked by, looked at me caringly, and said, "Everything will be fine." God used those brief words to lift my spirit and restore my confidence. Thank you, young man, whoever you are.

There is a time to be silent and a time to speak. Lord, help us to know the difference!

Appearance Can Be Deceiving

*As for those who seemed to be important—whatever they were
makes no difference to me;
God does not judge by external appearance.*
GALATIANS 2:6

It is a true story. There was this small community that had a gigantic oak tree in the middle of its town square. The tree was the pride of the townspeople. It had been there before most of them were born and would be there long after they were gone.

Then one day the unexpected happened. A storm hit the town and unleashed its fury on the giant oak tree. The trunk cracked in half and revealed the fact that the tree was eaten up on the inside with disease. A symbol of strength on the outside, it was weak and vulnerable on the inside. But no one knew until the storm came.

Jesus taught repeatedly that outward appearances can be deceiving. The Pharisees did a lot of "religious" stuff and deceived most folks, but Jesus saw right through them and said they were full of dead men's bones! The Bible says that while we tend to look on outward appearance, God always looks at the heart.

Bottom line: Let your life reflect outwardly what you are inwardly. Don't fake it. Don't create an image to be accepted by the religious establishment when that only forces you to cover up issues in your life you really need to deal with.

I think the story speaks a warning to all of us in the Christian camp about maintaining our personal relationship with Jesus

Christ and being persistent in the pursuit of holiness. Only daily time in the Word and in communication with the Father done in a spirit of humility, honesty, and openness will keep us authentic inside and out.

We have seen enough examples in the last few years of those who appeared to be mighty oaks later destroyed by a storm that revealed disease on the inside. None of us is immune from falling! And the disease of pride or indifference or greed or lust or . . . always begins on the inside and works its way out.

I have known some diseased oaks in my lifetime—people who disappointed me and left me feeling betrayed. But I have also known some truly authentic oaks who stood firm in the midst of the storms and revealed that Christ was the source of their lives. They leave for me a testimony to the grace of God and demonstrate the value of integrity.

Is the image you project to others the real you? If the storms were to hit today what would they reveal?

Less Stress, More Yield

Do not be anxious about anything, but in everything,
by prayer and petition, with thanksgiving,
present your requests to God. And the peace of God,
which transcends all understanding,
will guard your hearts and minds in Christ Jesus.
PHILIPPIANS 4:6–7

The TV commercial got my attention. The product they were promoting would, according to the announcer, help the farmer have a more plentiful harvest. Their slogan was: "Less stress, more yield." Maybe the reason those words caught my ear was that this was a time when I was dealing with a great deal of stress in my life. A test which they appropriately call the "stress test" verified the fact that the issues involved were indeed taking a toll on my physical health.

Most of you reading these words understand the effects of stress. We live with it daily. Some of us more than others, but none are exempt.

Let me say something that may shock you: Being a Christian does not make you stress-proof. In fact, being a Christian doesn't make you mistake-proof or accident-proof or anything-proof. Nor does it mean we automatically have great marriages or good relationships with the people in our lives. We have to take the principles of God's Word and *apply* them to our lives. That is a continual process. There are no "overnight successes" in the Christian life! That is why Jesus told us to *abide* in Him and *do* His Word. Paul exhorts us to *keep on* being filled with the Spirit.

The enemy of our soul is relentless in his attacks, and the pressures of life will not go away. The more responsibility we carry, the greater the stress level. While it is unlikely that my stress or yours will disappear, there are creative ways of dealing with it. In my case, that meant a low-fat diet, exercise, and some attitude adjustments. I needed to learn to cast my cares on the One who is able to carry them and stop trying to meet my needs in my own strength.

Prayer is a very effective stress remover. And that is one way we can minister to those around us who are stressed out. I cannot begin to tell you how uplifting and liberating the prayers of fellow believers have been in my life. Stress doesn't mean we aren't spiritual; it is simply evidence of the fact that we live in a fallen society. Learning to cast our cares on the Lord and putting a priority on our time of communion with Him will go a long way toward producing less stress and more yield in our lives!